Cyber-Nationalism in China

Cyber-Nationalism in China

Challenging Western media portrayals of Internet censorship in China

by

Ying Jiang

Discipline of Media, The University of Adelaide, South Australia

UNIVERSITY OF
ADELAIDE PRESS

THE UNIVERSITY
of ADELAIDE

Published in Adelaide by

University of Adelaide Press
The University of Adelaide
Level 1, 230 North Terrace
South Australia
5005
press@adelaide.edu.au
www.adelaide.edu.au/press

The University of Adelaide Press publishes externally refereed scholarly books by staff of the University of Adelaide. It aims to maximise the accessibility to its best research by publishing works through the internet as free downloads and as high quality printed volumes on demand.

Electronic Index: this book is available from the website as a down-loadable PDF with fully searchable text. Please use the electronic version to serve as the index.

For the full Cataloguing-in-Publication data please contact the National Library of Australia: cip@nla.gov.au

Cyber-nationalism in China: challenging western media portrayals of internet censorship in China / by Ying Jiang.

I   Internet — Social aspects — China
II   Internet — Political aspects — China
III   Internet — Censorship
IV   Nationalism — China

1.   Jiang, Ying

ISBN (paperback) 978-0-9871718-4-9
ISBN (ebook) 978-0-9871718-9-4

Project Editor: Patrick Allington
Cover design: Emma Spoehr
Book design: Zoë Stokes

Contents

List of Tables and Figures

Tables

Figures

Acknowledgements

I would like to express my gratitude to the following people who provided support, talked things over, read, wrote, offered comments: Dr Michael Wilmore, Associate Professor Mary Griffiths, Dr Peter Pugsley, Dr Chika Anyanwu, Dr Sal Humphrey, Professor John Taplin. My special thanks go to Associate Professor Jill Burton, who read the whole manuscript several times, provided valuable comments and excellent editing service. Dr Patrick Allington, Dr John Emerson and Zoë Stokes provided critical remarks of great help.

I am also thankful to those anonymous reviewers who made many interesting comments and drew my attention to issues I had originally neglected.

My heartfelt thanks go to extended family for their ongoing support: Jiangen Jiang and Lan Wang (my parents); Chunhua Yang and Xiangdong Wang (my parents-in-law), and; Jimmy Rugari and Holly Lau (my best friends in Adelaide). Being the only daughter and the only daughter-in-law who lives far away from my parents and parents-in-law, I am in much emotional debt to all of them for my absences on their birthdays, anniversaries and those days when they were sick. Above all, this book is dedicated to the most important man in my life: Michael Yijun Wang, my husband, for making tremendous sacrifices and having the courage to embark on this long and winding academic journey with me.

Preface

I am one of China's Generation Y. I had a joyful childhood, heavy-burdened school life and physical comfort when I grew up. I cannot clearly recall what China was like when I was little, but I clearly remember the doubts that China left in the little girl growing up. For instance, I wondered why news on TV always displayed a happy China while I could see that people around me were suffering. Why, when people complained about certain things on the dinner table, were they always told: "Be cautious. " I wasn't brave enough to ask anyone to satisfy my curiosity at that time because I was one of the "outstanding model students" at school. Being a model student, you were not expected to ask questions irrelevant to your study.

In 2000, I stood on "Western" land for the first time in my life. I went to England for a higher degree. As a spoiled post-80s young person who had rarely done any housework at home, I had to learn everything from changing quilt-covers to feeding myself. I felt lonely in a foreign land and the Internet proved to be my best friend; from talking to people back home to doing research for my essays, I wouldn't have been able to live without the Internet. What I experienced during my stay in the UK contradicted most of my previous understandings of the West, and my Internet searches provided me with answers to my earlier doubts.

I went back to China once a year. During the summer holiday in 2004, my hometown looked beautiful, and it had changed in just one year. My relatives had more money; they could afford expensive clothes, watches, even private cars, things which years ago they had never imagined owning. My cousins were happily addicted to the Internet with a new fashion — blogging — something they understood as an online diary. They were basically recording what they had done on the weekend and what they had bought recently, how hard the school exams and boring their jobs were.

Back in the UK, I came across a journal article that stated that blogging might bring down China's Internet censorship. Instinctively, I perceived that this Western argument was overly optimistic. But before I indulged myself in analyzing this unjustified optimism, I noticed an even more fascinating phenomenon: my friends and relatives in China were not greatly concerned about limited individual freedoms of speech. In contrast, they were more bothered by attention from the West, and they expressed their unhappiness about this in their blogs.

My interest in Chinese bloggers' attitudes towards the Western media was stimulated by their complaints in 2005. But my passion to study Chinese bloggers' attitudes was considerably strengthened by the Great Chinese Censorship Hoax in 2006 when two Chinese bloggers, by suddenly shutting down their own sites, fooled some Western media into thinking their postings were being censored by the Chinese government.

In 2008, due to the Tibetan unrest and the Olympic torch relay, Chinese bloggers' anger rose to a historical height. In August 2008, I was fortunate to be selected as one of "The 100 Outstanding Young Chinese Leaders in the World" in the organizers' category "a Chinese youth from Australia" by the Dragon Foundation based in Hong Kong. The chosen 100 young ethnic Chinese, who came from all over the world, received a ten-day study trip in the Pearl River delta region of China. My passion to investigate Chinese bloggers' anger became even stronger after this trip because during it I had opportunities to talk not only to the other 99 delegates, of whom 20 were from mainland China, but also to chat to the local Chinese youth who had volunteered to smooth our journey. There was laughter when we compared experiences — such as the cost of buying Estée Lauder skin care products in Australia and in China, the number of QQ friends we had, the blog entries we liked reading — until I touched on the topic of what the others thought of the West. The volunteers then lectured me, expressing overwhelming anger about distorted Western coverage, and tried passionately to save me from being "brainwashed by Western media".

In my view, all the experiences we shared added to the importance of analyzing the issue of Chinese bloggers' anger. I needed to know what the underlying elements were that had fostered the political passion of this particular generation who, otherwise apathetic towards politics, were now ignited by what they saw as unwarranted, negative coverage of China by the Western media.

There can be no such thing as a neutral judge, despite attempts by someone such as me to do away with an "us" and "them" binary. Instead, I have aimed in this book to illustrate and critique the dominant trends and themes the topic lends itself to and hence provide an insightful perspective on an unusual phenomenon.

To this end, as a Chinese researcher in an English-speaking academic setting, I used both Chinese and English scholarly works, translating into English any Chinese materials included as evidence unless otherwise indicated.

Due to the nature of this research topic, I have used the Internet extensively. Internet sources normally have no page numbers, which causes confusion when direct quotations are used. Quotations in the text from Internet sources I therefore cite by name and date followed by "n.p." (meaning "no pagination"). Internet sources appear in the Bibliography at the end of the book.

PART I

Democratic Differences between China and the West

This is a struggle of resistance against western hegemonic discourse. We need to fully recognize that this will be a long-term, difficult and complex battle. But regardless of the outcome, we all firmly believe: western nations' days of using several of their crap media in an absurd attempt to fool people with their rotten words will soon be over for good!

(Original text posted on http://www.anti-cnn.com/index2.html in Chinese [Translation, John Kennedy, Global Voices Online, 24 March 2008])

1

一

Introduction

A difference of opinion

A recent blogging conflict between Western media and young people in China who displayed intense anger at how the West was evaluating China provided the catalyst for this book. The development of tension between Chinese bloggers and Western media has highlighted a major difference in the understanding of the natures of nationalism and censorship between China and the West. The notion of "the West", too, is open to interpretation. The term has specific reference in the blogging conflict featured in this book. By it, Chinese Internet users mean the UK and USA mainly. The reasons are historical and linguistic. These two countries were the leading countries of the Eight Power Allied Forces that invaded China on 7 September 1901. The other six were France, Germany, Japan, Russia, Austria and Italy, non-English speaking nations whose languages do not operate as world languages on the Internet. In this book, I follow the bloggers' understanding of 'Western' while understanding that the term has other broader meanings.

By the time of the blogging conflict, China had already captured global attention owing to its recent accelerated pace of market-based economic reform and accompanying high rates of economic growth. Discussion of political reforms that might follow the economic development paralleled the commentaries on the historic economic changes. These discussions converged with debates about the increasing use of the Internet in China, because growth in the use of these new media and communication technologies has depended upon both economic and political change.

When China established its market economy, those observers who believe political pluralism accompanies economic liberalization predicted that China's market forces would eventually change the country's one-party system (Cherrington 1991; Francis 1989; Rosen 1991, 1992; Sun 1991). China's embrace of the Internet led to the popular assumption in the West that the Internet would ultimately be a force for democracy in China. However, such transformation is still an unrealized dream (Pei 2006a & 2006b). Research in various disciplines shows that non-liberal regimes such as China have been successful in containing the use of the Internet (Boas & Kalathil 2003, p. 140; Abbott 2001; Goldsmith & Wu 2006, p. 28; Kurlantzick 2004). More importantly, these twin forces of the market and the Internet may actually add a new direction and strength to the strategies that China employs to regulate Chinese citizens' relations with the nation-state and the wider world. Engaging with the state and the wider world, while constituting new ways for Chinese citizens to construct a national identity, has also caused tensions among the forces for Chinese liberalization and government control of markets: this is evident in existing political discourse. It appears that Western commentators on these tensions in Chinese affairs are fixated on one major question: is the use of the Internet leading to political change in China?

However, their focus on this question of how China is to develop its own version of cyberspace and, in so doing, its own political future has caused an outburst of anger from Chinese bloggers towards the Western media that provide the main platforms for such commentary. In particular, over-zealous attention to censorship issues in China and Chinese bloggers' angry responses to this attention has recently led to Chinese bloggers' widespread resentment of all Western coverage of sensitive issues in China. Examples of the general pattern of this tension are easy to identify: Western media expose Chinese censorship (Usher 2006), Chinese bloggers then slam Western media bias (Massagemilk 2006); Western media criticize the Chinese crackdown on Tibet, Chinese bloggers then allege Western media distortion (Kongqixibo 2009); the Western media debate boycotting the Beijing Olympics to oppose the human-rights situation in China, Chinese bloggers then describe the Western media as arrogant towards China (Lingfengwangzi 2008).

The prevailing consumerism in Chinese cyberspace is a growing element of Chinese culture and an important aspect of this book. Chinese bloggers, who have strongly embraced consumerism and tend to be apathetic about politics, have nonetheless demonstrated political passion over issues such as the Western media's negative coverage of China. In this book, I focus upon this passion — Chinese bloggers' angry reactions to the Western media's coverage of censorship issues in current China — in order to examine China's current potential for political reform. A central focus of this book, then, is the specific issue of censorship and how to interpret the Chinese characteristics of it as a mechanism currently used to maintain state control.

While this book examines fundamental questions surrounding the political implications of the Internet in China, it avoids simply predicting that the Internet does or does not lead to democratization. Applying a theoretical approach based on the Foucauldian notion of governmentality, the book builds on current scholarship that has attempted to move beyond examining the dynamics of the socio-cultural and -political use of new media technologies (Tai 2007; Yu 2007; Yang 2009; Zheng 2008). Instead, this book's more intricate theoretical approach does not only accommodate the kind of liberal (apolitical or political) use observed on the Internet in China, but indicates that desires for political change, such as they are, are implicitly embedded in the relationship between China's online communities and state apparatus — noting, however, that the latter claims total governance over the Internet in the name of the people.

Furthermore, the analysis in this book distinguishes between different meanings of political change, namely, liberalization and democratization (O'Donnell & Schmitter 1986, p. 6). I argue that China's cyberspace displays only early signs of political liberalization. The desire for the structural changes required for political democratization remains low or dormant in most of China's Internet users. The Chinese government's endorsement of limited forms of personal empowerment via specific topics existing uncensored online is a governance strategy, one Foucault (1988a & 1991) labels a technology of the self. Since it is permitted and operates through self-regulation, it minimizes the need for direct political and/or policing intervention, and, indirectly, it produces what can be called controlled self-managing consumers (Powell & Cook 2007).

This book examines the political implications of China's Generation Y Internet usage. This young generation forms the majority of Chinese bloggers and Internet users, and will furnish China's leaders in the near future (Stanat 2006). The analysis employs Foucault's notions of governmentality and technologies of the self. With new evidence from case studies, I aim not only to reemphasize the differences between prevailing prescriptive assumptions about the usage of the Internet in China and its supposed Chinese characteristics, but also to investigate why some areas of Chinese cyberspace are more liberalized than others. Besides, I examine the different roles of young Chinese in shaping the character of the free discussion areas, which do exist on the Web.

This study illuminates the strengths and weaknesses in existing research on the political implications of Internet usage in China and demonstrates the need for more socio-culturally engaged analyses. Most of all, it demonstrates how there can be liberal areas of activity in a country such as China without the state abandoning its overall non-liberal characteristics; the many contradictory discourses in and about China begin to make sense once the politics and governmentality of so-called free online spaces in China are understood.

Internet use in China

Western netizens see the Internet as a tool for free speech and the advancement of democracy in non-liberal regimes. The majority of Chinese bloggers do not see the need for this — witness their anger at Western commentary on Chinese political actions in the first decade of this century. Chinese bloggers' angry reactions also illustrate the different societal values in China at large and Western democracies — in particular, the gap between political reality and Western assumptions of the power of the Internet in China. This gap in understanding stimulated the focus of this book.

Common assumptions about the political potential of the Internet

Observers have predicted the democratizing potential of the Internet since the beginning of the 1980s (Barber 1998; Grossman 1995). The advent of the Internet was seen as a precursor to the break-up of dictatorships and their shift to democracy and the strengthening of freedoms for citizens in established democracies (Shapiro 1999). For example, in 1996, the legendary libertarian and musician John Perry Barlow authored the utopian text "A Declaration of Independence in Cyberspace". It declared:

In China, Germany, France, Russia, Singapore, Italy and the United States, you are trying to ward off the virus of liberty by erecting guard posts at the frontiers of Cyberspace. These may keep out the contagion for a small time, but they will not work in a world that will soon be blanketed in bit-bearing media. (Barlow 1996)

But although cyber libertarians believed the Internet would strengthen existing democracies or turn non-democratic regimes into democracies, sceptics counter-argued that this technology could also reinforce surveillance (Gandy 1993; Lyon 2003, p. 80). Meanwhile the development of the Internet in China has picked up pace exponentially and the amount of research into its role in facilitating democratization has grown. These developments have stimulated debate as to whether the Internet will generate more public discussion of the real potential for democratic reform in China, and some commentators believe the current levels and range of discussion may in any case facilitate some political liberalization in China (Browning 2002; Ferdinand 2000; Gutstein 1999; Saco 2002; Simon, Corrales & Wolfensberger 2002; Shane 2004). Indeed, this belief is widely held in the West, where the Internet is believed to be ultimately a force for democracy. Former US President Bill Clinton went as far as predicting that the Chinese government's crackdown on the Internet in China would be "like trying to nail Jello to the wall" (Clinton 2000). The hearings held before the US House of Representatives in February 2006 by representatives of Google, Microsoft, Yahoo! and Cisco also reflected this widespread assumption (US House of Representatives 2006), which is based on what has happened elsewhere.

In the Mexican state of Chiapas, for example, rebels — the Zapatista Army of National Liberation — used information technology to great effect in order to protest against the central government. Since 1994, the ZANL has been in a declared war against the Mexican state. From the beginning, the ZANL has made communication with the rest of Mexico and the world a high priority. It has used modern technology, including cellular phones and the Internet, to generate international solidarity with sympathetic people and organizations (Castells 1997, p. 80).

The people of Indonesia also used the Internet cleverly in their efforts to bring down the Suharto regime (Hill & Sen 2005). With the ability to provide alternative information and opportunities for dialogues that are free from the intervention of the state, the Internet became a potential aid to democratization in Indonesia. Although the Internet might not be the only tool that caused the political revolution, there is no doubt that without it Suharto's regime could have continued more easily to suppress dissent (Lim 2006).

In Egypt, the organization of protests against the existing regime included significant use of the Internet (Fitzgerald 2011). In January 2011, the outage and protests were initiated by Facebook users within the country before the government shut down the Internet. In the following month, the 30-year government of Hosni Mubarak ended with relatively little bloodshed. It is indisputable that the Internet and social media played a vital role. In fact, the revolution may not have happened at all without the Internet.

York (2011) suggests that in Tunisia, freeing up the country's Internet was the first step toward a democratic ideal. The Jasmine Revolution in Tunisia is also called the Facebook Revolution. Facebook posts, tweets, blog entries and e-mails mobilized weeks of protests across the North African country of Tunisia against the autocratic regime of the long-time president, fueled by a young, Internet-savvy generation of bloggers.

Based on such examples, some observers continue to predict that non-liberal regimes struggle once the Internet technology has been introduced. Certainly, wider availability of the Internet raises the prospect of strategic threats to national identity. The Internet and cyberspace mean borderless communication opportunities for dissidents, effective mobilization of domestic opposition, and increased opportunities to collect information about alternative political systems (Lagerkvist 2006, p. 16). These threats have, as predicted (Ferdinand, 2000, p. 12) become more severe in non-democratic countries.

However, pessimists can counter-claim that China and some other non-liberal regimes have so far been successful in their endeavours to "nail the jello to the wall" (Lagerkvist 2006, p. 17). With evidence from non-liberal nations that simultaneously develop the Internet and successfully prevent its use it as a base for political opposition (Boas & Kalathil 2003), new media studies have reason to remain cautious about the Internet's allegedly democratic potential in non-liberal countries.

Meanwhile, it remains uncontroversial that the Internet filtering system in China is the most sophisticated in the world (Deibert et al. 2008). In fact, the boom of the Internet in China prompted an increasing number of studies early this century on the censorship and the filtering system of the Internet in China (Baker 2001; Chase 2002; Foster 2000; Hughes 2003; Kalathil 2001; Mengin 2004; Miller 2002; Woesler & Zhang 2002; Xi 2006; Zhou 2005). Several academic institutions continue empirical analysis of China's Internet filtering, including the Citizen Lab at the Munk Centre for International Studies, University of Toronto; the Berkman Center for Internet and Society at Harvard Law School; and the Advanced Network Research Group at the Cambridge Security Programme (Centre for International Studies) at the University of Cambridge (Deibert et al. 2008, p. 3). The most comprehensive and up to date report, "Internet Filtering in China", was published online on 15 June 2009 by The Open Net Initiative, which is a collaborative partnership among these three leading academic institutions (ONI 2009).

Researchers have ultimately found it hard to predict political outcomes from widespread use of cyberspace. For although scholarship and technical research on the Internet in China started indicating the need for a more sober view of the liberating force of the Internet in China after witnessing the Chinese government's successful control of it, the flourishing of Chinese blogging still encourages the optimistic view that the Internet might ultimately be a force for political change (Goldsmith & Wu 2006; Zhao 2006). Nicholas Kristof of *The New York Times* even went so far as to predict in his article "Death by a thousand blogs" that "it's the Chinese leadership itself that is digging the Communist Party's grave, by giving the Chinese people broadband" (Kristof 2005). Other researchers also remain optimistic about the Internet's potential. Wang (2008, p. 164) argues that in a country like China, where the Internet is under tight surveillance, new citizen media such as blogging has a bright future, and Albow and Holland (2008, p. 263) used China as a case study to demonstrate the liberalizing implications of the blogosphere.

The Internet's Chinese characteristics

The debate on the political implications of the Internet predominantly tells us the Internet can be a tool both for democratization and its containment. The posing of this tense binary opposition of control versus liberalization is of general interest to mainstream social science theory because "so many theorists assume that China's democratization should follow established trajectories of democratic development" (Lagerkvist 2006, p. 18). China, however, is developing an unexpected, off-course pathway according to the conventional theories of democratization, modernization and globalization. Since the Chinese reality does not conform to established models of thought, the Chinese situation is invariably explained as something that is rare or exceptional, or trapped in transition. Therefore current scholarship has moved far beyond making simple predictions and is examining the more subtle dynamics and patterns of socio-cultural and -political uses of this new media technology through a focus on the new collective practices and activism in Chinese cyberspace (Yang 2009; Zheng 2008).

I hold that although the Chinese situation can be described as transitional it is also exceptional. For the foreseeable future, at least until China's Generation Y takes power, the political changes in the forms currently experienced in Western liberal contexts cannot be expected in China. Although media spaces that were restricted to apolitical and consumerist commentary now also embrace political content, political discussions are mainly pro-China.

It is nonetheless true that blogging in China is popular and that its popularity suggests early signs, at least, of political liberalization in Chinese cyberspace. The Chinese blogosphere does enjoy a certain degree of autonomy and freedom from censorship. Certainly, some of what previously would have been termed incorrect political ideology is nowadays more tolerated in the Chinese blogosphere. However, political liberalization is not the same thing as political democratization. For this reason alone, the possibility of structural change in current China cannot be described as high. Although the Internet has been a democratic tool in other political settings, it can also be a tool for the containment of democracy. The Internet is only one among many tools or factors in the development of democratic structures (Lagervist 2006, p. 18). Other factors such as the socio-cultural context, ideological control and leadership are equally significant. Thus, the potential democratizing impact of the Internet needs to be substantiated against other factors and located within a larger range of circumstances, such as socio-political forces for nationalism and governance strategies. This book therefore focuses on examining the political implications of the Internet in China by concentrating on the larger, more fundamental factors concerned, namely, the discourses of nationalism, censorship, and governmentality, and how they have uniquely combined to influence the particular pathway that China appears to have embarked upon.

A different political pathway

The unexpected reactions of the Chinese bloggers in the episode examined in this book indicate that China as a whole is not keen to make the political changes needed to create the liberalism that many in the West are hoping to see in Chinese society.

Of course, the anger towards the Western media analyzed in this study does not represent all generations in China; it is a phenomenon concentrated amongst China's Generation Y, which has extensive access to the Internet and in general blogs. These young people are proud of China's accomplishments, and together they form "a group whose solipsistic tendencies have been further encouraged by a growing obsession with consumerism" (Elegant 2007). I chose this particular generational focus for my analysis for two reasons:

1. Generation Y embraced Western consumer culture rapidly, having grown up with the Internet. It was this generation that many Western media commentators predicted to threaten the continuing governance of the Chinese Communist Party (CCP) and was the most likely to oppose Internet censorship, and that, ultimately, these two factors would lead to more democratization in China.

2. Based on the distinctive social characteristics of this generation, however, structural change in China does not seem likely to occur soon.

For better understanding of the second factor, Chapter 2 provides an analysis of the idiosyncratic social characteristics of this particular, young Chinese generation. My main concern in the following section, however, is to document the development of the anger felt by many Chinese bloggers, and to define the boundaries of the anger I examine in this book.

The development of anger

Based on a succession of remarkable events in China over a four-year period, I categorize the development of that anger in three phases: 2005, 2006, and 2008.

Phase one, 2005

Chinese bloggers' complaints about the Western media started with the famous Chinese blogger Wang Jianshuo, who was interviewed by the BBC in 2005. After the interview, Wang posted his displeasure at the BBC on his blog:

> BBC interview=censorship question interview.
>
> There are too many pre-defined questions like censorship and BBC is trying to find piece of information, filter it and create an exciting picture for people in the "civilized" world. (Wang 2005)

In his blog, Wang also mentioned several other Chinese bloggers who endorsed his displeasure, for example Issac Mao and Yining, who also had had the experience of Western media interviews. Yining said:

> Rabiya, BBC, and all the big media:
>
> Do NOT set the interviewees up, do NOT use the interviewees, do NOT manipulate them by cornering them and directing them to the opinions you yourself want to present, so to fit into your own political agenda. So if that's what you are doing, sorry, there is

no way I can cooperate. Tonight, it's not about censorship, but fair and professional reporting. Censorship is another game, we will play it another day. (Wang 2005)

Wang also quoted the organizer of Chinese Bloggers Conference, Issac Mao's expression of his experience with the BBC:

The reporter who called me asked whether I can speak on the LIVE program for BBC this evening London time. She was preparing the issue to be broadcast tonight at 6:45 AM [PM] London time. The topic will be the China Blogger Conference. I am pretty sure the topic will be around censorship again. I think the time is just too early for me. It is so easy to convert Greenwich Mean Time to Shanghai time, since one is GMT +0 and Shanghai is GMT +8. So I said I prefer to have a better sleep other than wake up at 4:00 AM in the morning. The other reason is, just as the previous interview, I was not 100% comfortable when I am approached with a pre-defined conclusion and my role is just to be an evidence to support the idea. That is neither interesting nor meaningful. (Wang 2005)

In addition to Wang, an anonymous Chinese blogger posted an article about Yining's interview invitation on Chinatopblog:

No surprise, BBC asked their eternal theme — censorship in China. It was heard that BBC interviewed hundreds of people about this topic in their program, Yining is one of them. However Yining is a wise man, he avoided the trap. BBC commented Yining "self-censored". Oh, brother, BBC made us sick. They are more like unjust judges than reporters. I feel no wrong for what I have done. (Anonymous 2005)

But these fragmentary statements did not get the main attention of the Western media until the Great Chinese Censorship Hoax of March 2006.

Phase two, 2006

On 8 March 2006, Chinese-language blogs Massage Milk and Milk Pig made the same announcements that "Due to unavoidable reasons with which everyone is familiar, this blog is temporarily closed" (Goldkorn 2006). Bloggers and journalists in the West spread the message that the closure was another crackdown by the Chinese government (Fowler & Qin 2006). For example, the BBC news website commented that this act was a government crackdown (Usher 2006). French free-press group *Reporters Sans Frontieres* also condemned the shutdowns of the blogs in a statement (Fowler & Qin 2006). But it turned out to be a hoax. Both those two blogs were back up and running after a day. Wang Xiaofeng, the author of the Massage Milk blog, explained in an interview that in shutting down his blog he wanted "to make a point about freedom of speech — just one directed at the West instead of at Beijing" (Fowler & Qin 2006). He told Interfax:

I just wanted to make fun of Western journalists … Doesn't need to be serious on the Internet. I don't like it that Western media take a distorted view of China, though China does have problems. I thought that if I closed my blog, it would stir their imagination and then they would begin blah blah. It really is as expected. So let they [Western journalists] have an April Fool's day in advance. (MacKinnon 2006)

Later on, the BBC corrected its original story, which indicated the Chinese government's involvement in the shutdown of blogs, and *Reporters Sans Frontieres* modified its statement on March 9 by calling the shutdown a joke (Fowler & Qin 2006). Wang Xiaofeng described the Western press as irresponsible: "the hoax was designed to give foreign media a lesson that Chinese affairs are not always the way you think" (Fowler & Qin 2006).

This hoax demonstrates Chinese bloggers' resentment of Western criticism of Chinese censorship issues. Two years later, in 2008, this resentment expanded to the West's generally negative coverage of China; this time their anger attracted the attention of the world.

Phase three, 2008

By 2008, Chinese bloggers' antipathy towards the Western media had reached a peak. At this time their extreme anger was inflamed by the CNN news commentator Jack Cafferty, who described Chinese products as junk and Chinese people as goons and thugs on CNN's political programme 'The Situation Room' on 9 April:

> We continue to import their junk with the lead paint on them and the poisoned pet food and export, you know, jobs to places where you can pay workers a dollar a month to turn out the stuff that we're buying from Wal-Mart. So I think our relationship with China has certainly changed. I think they're basically the same bunch of goons and thugs they've been for the last 50 years. (Mostrous 2008)

Following Cafferty's comments, about 6000 Chinese Americans and overseas Chinese students gathered outside CNN's studios in Los Angeles protesting his comments, demanding CNN apologize to Chinese people and calling for Cafferty's dismissal (MacKinnon 2008).

Shortly after, in the middle of April 2008, some YouTube videos and Facebook groups criticized CNN's coverage of the situation in Lhasa, Tibet. Chinese bloggers claimed that

Figure 1.1: Photos of 2008 Tibetan rioters (Left: Used by CNN; Right: Original Version)
Source: http://rconversation.blogs.com/rconversation/2008/03/anti-cnn-the-me.html (accessed 20 June 2009)

CNN.com had manipulated the photo of Tibetan rioters (MacKinnon 2008). The picture used by CNN displayed a military vehicle chasing protesters (see Figure 1, left); the original version showed a different scenario, in which Tibetan rioters appear to be attacking military vehicles (see Figure 1, right). Chinese bloggers argued that CNN manipulated the photo intentionally to tell a particular story.

Together with Cafferty's inflammatory comments, this controversial photo led to the establishment of a website called "anti-CNN" by a Chinese blogger. In 2008, the website stated:

> We are not against the Western media, but against the lies and fabricated stories in the media. We are not against the Western people, but against the prejudice from the Western society" (Anti-CNN 2008c).

> The website claims that the Western media's misidentifications were intentional, part of an agenda of the Western media. (Zuckerman 2008).

Further postings explain:

> For a long time now, certain western media, best represented by CNN and BBC, in the name of press freedom have been unscrupulously slandering and defaming developing nations. In order to achieve their unspoken goal, they mislead and they ensnare, switching black for white, confusing right and wrong, fabricating … willing to go to any length. (Translation by Kennedy 2008)

The anger against the Western media then spread throughout Chinese cyberspace, reaching an extremely high level among Chinese bloggers. The average comments posted on the anti-CNN forum overwhelmingly expressed anger at Western media-biased coverage and continued to intensify. The website "Anti-CNN" changed its name to "April Youth". It continues to supply textual, photographic, audio and video examples that display North American and European media's perceptions of the situation in China. These perceptions, the Chinese bloggers maintain, are misrepresentations. For example:

> This is a struggle of resistance against western hegemonic discourse. We need to fully recognize that this will be a long-term, difficult and complex battle. But regardless of the outcome, we all firmly believe: Western nations' days of using several of their crap media in an absurd attempt to fool people with their rotten words will soon be over for good! (Kennedy 2008)

The research focus

Chinese bloggers have been angered by what they perceive as the bias of the Western media. This bias appears to be of two types: firstly, there is the bias concerning censorship, such as the BBC's interview questions in 2005 and *Reporters Sans Frontieres'* condemnation of the censorship hoax in 2006; secondly, there is bias in images of how the nation is perceived, such as Caffery's comments and CNN's coverage on Tibet in 2008. The anger I examine in this book specifically focuses on the first category, yet the two categories are related. The anger that was inflamed by Western criticism of Chinese censorship practices is closely linked to

Western fundamental beliefs about the democratizing potential of the Internet and, therefore, national governance. There are two reasons for the perspective taken in this book.

First, there is the intrinsic significance of the research. Blogging has flourished alongside the recent rapid development of the Internet in China. As a phenomenon, this calls for up-to-date empirical research examining the democratic potential of the Internet in China. Indeed, the focus on Chinese bloggers' hostility towards Western criticism of Chinese censorship practices contributes new understanding to the puzzle of Chinese nationalism. Previous studies of Chinese nationalism have largely explained questions of national identity and national image using the usual West/China and Japan/China dichotomies (Delanty & Kumar 2006; Gries 2005; Hughes 2006; Karl 2002; Wang 1996), although there are some exceptions to this trend. Some scholars have paid attention to the complex interrelationship in China among nationalism, the state, and democratizing forces (Chang 1998; Friedman 1997; He & Guo 2000, Yu 1996; Sautman 1997). These scholars have pointed out that when it comes to problems over national boundaries, Chinese nationalism normally conflicts with democratic goals. Most of them, however, take Chinese citizens' desire for democracy for granted and ascribe the recent anti-democracy trend to the intervention of the Communist Party. This interpretation enables them to still admit the democratic potential of nationalism in China (Harris 2002; He & Guo 2000; Wang 2003).

Nevertheless, the wave of Chinese bloggers' nationalism in the middle of the first decade of the twenty-first century has shaken earlier assessments in the West of modern China's potential for democratic reform. My examination of Chinese bloggers' anger challenges Western assumptions about how, and whether, democracy can develop during heightened periods of nationalist loyalty. Moreover, this examination unveils new, different characteristics of Chinese nationalism, namely, the young generation's distrust of democracy and consequent apathy towards further political reforms. This new phenomenon, then, contests the potential for democracy in China and offers new interdisciplinary insights into nationalism and governmentality, particularly in relation to China.

Second, then, Chinese bloggers' anger at Western media criticism of censorship practices in their homeland is a research topic which, while manageable and interesting in itself, is, as I have argued above, capable of deepening the understanding of the larger issues of Chinese nationalism and the country's potential for democratic reform.

As an initial step to my research, I carried out a preliminary investigation. For one month (18 April to 18 May 2008) I collected Chinese bloggers' daily posts on anti-CNN forums about Western coverage of Tibetan issues. The data were immediately interesting, since they raised questions concerning the criteria the Chinese bloggers were using to establish Western bias. I compared the Western reports during this period with those on Chinese CCTV news and other Chinese media and discovered that Chinese bloggers were categorizing three types of coverage as biased according to the following three lines of argument:

1. If news reported by the Western media is not reported by the Chinese media, then the Western media are biased because the news stories are false and the Western media is claimed to be racist. For example:

> <u>Sample No. 71</u> (26/04) *Follow up — the story of the American being attacked is fake*
> Anti-CNN members' comments: Couldn't be confirmed on Chinese domestic media, therefore it's another distortion.

2. If negative news reported by the Western media is also reported by the Chinese media, then the Western media are biased because they are focused on the "inevitable flaws". For example:

> <u>Sample No. 55</u> (26/04) *CNN's anti-Chinese campaign: CNN special: made in China*
> Anti-CNN members' comments: It's biased — CNN focus on the inevitable flaws.

3. If positive news reported by the Chinese media is not reported by the Western media, then the Western media are biased. For example:

> <u>Sample No. 60</u> (18/04) *Pictures in China, but not yet in the West (3) — Lhasa*
> Anti-CNN members' comments: Biased Western media — because the pro-China photos in CCTV not shown in the Western media.

Clearly, the Chinese bloggers' criteria necessitated deeper investigation into how China and the West differently conceive the roles of media and communication, especially since the clash between Western and Chinese media protocols, which began with their conception, has proven impervious to increasing globalization (see also Hachten & Hachten 1996, p. 13). However, this book does not have the scope to fully articulate these socio-cultural and -political conflicts nor to thoroughly investigate differences over online censorship issues in China. However, the long-term causes of young people's anger at perceived criticisms of China's national image go far beyond any immediate conflicts over the roles of media or communication in enabling or limiting freedoms of speech, which is the focus of this book. So, since socio-cultural and -political issues are connected to online censorship, the book does shed some light on them insofar as they relate to nationalistic sentiment.

The nationalism this book deals with does not directly impinge on issues such as national borderline disputes; it rather addresses how domestic political decisions affect individuals, their agency and their freedom of expression. This focus, employing cases such as the Chinese bloggers' heightened national loyalty in reaction to Western media criticism of national censorship practices, elucidates important working relationships between the nation-state and individuals. Fine-grained analyses of specific cases such as this provide insight into the astonishingly successful balance of power between the non-liberal Communist regime and Generation Y, which is more in touch with the sorts of freedoms enjoyed in the West than has ever been possible for a young generation in China before.

Different attitudes

Importantly, this book suggests there is a difference of attitude not only between the West and China but also between this young Chinese generation, Generation Y, and its predecessors. China's well-known Internet censorship practices, considered a threat to freedom of expression in the West, seem not to be so in the minds of many young Chinese bloggers, whose national loyalty, ironically, has only been enflamed by Western surveillance.

This astonishing phenomenon has not been comprehensively studied by either Western or Chinese researchers. There has also been little journalistic coverage of the issue, apart from that of Fowler and Qin (2006) who exposed Chinese bloggers' shut-down hoax early in 2006. In contrast, there was much discussion of the hoax on the Chinese Internet: for example, "Massage milk hoax and 'peer pressure' in Western media" (Bingfeng 2006), "Massage Milk and the disaster of journalism in China" (Goldkorn 2006), "Massage Milk censored" (Alex 2006), and "The great Chinese censorship hoax" by MacKinnon (2006), a researcher of Chinese blogs based at Hong Kong's Chinese University.

Most online discussions on Chinese bloggers' anger, however, concern how their anger is represented. They don't dissect it or explore its underlying causes. Only a few discussions have related the anger to fundamental political differences between the West and China. In "Newsweek and Time: a tale of two China cover stories" Goldkorn (2006) assumes "very, very few people are blogging for revolution or radical change in China". Likewise in "The great censorship hoax", MacKinnon (2006) argues

> Blogs are not going to bring down the CCP, and it's absolutely true that Chinese bloggers are frustrated by the focus on censorship to the exclusion of much else that's very exciting about the Chinese blogosphere.

MacKinnon is one of few scholars who link Chinese bloggers' anger to wider considerations such as the political implications of the Internet in China. She points out (2007) that Westerners are surprised that Chinese bloggers don't see themselves as "victims who are waiting to be liberated" (p. 42). She argues that blogging in China is more likely to encourage political evolution than revolution. MacKinnon is also one of the very few who have noted the Chinese characteristic of autonomous censorship online (2009a), observing that the censorship mechanisms in the Chinese blogosphere are decentralized to the extent that individual and private company action continue to markedly affect the balance between freedom and control online.

However, as noted, MacKinnon's research is untypical. As a result, there is as yet only fragmentary understanding of what autonomous censorship represents in China and the tension between Western media and Chinese bloggers regarding Chinese Internet censorship issues continues. What most explanations fail to include in their discussions are consideration of, first, the distinctive new wave of nationalistic sentiment among China's Generation Y, and, second, Chinese government tactics (governmentality) in shaping this generation's expression of nationalism, that goes beyond what can be described as a propaganda strategy. These underlying issues are crucial factors in assessing the likelihood for imminent structural change in how China is governed. They are why I chose to compile blogging data so as to analyze Chinese anger, the symptom of the major misunderstandings between the West and China over Chinese characteristic Internet usage and its general meaning for China politically.

My aim was to understand not only some of the political implications of the Internet in a Chinese context but also the CCP's skilful encouragement and management of Internet usage. In doing so, my book is able to point out the complex relationship between nationalism and consumerism in Chinese cyberspace and argue that the government, in promoting consumerism and all the interaction that goes with it, has granted Chinese bloggers freedom of speech in some ways. The resulting online discourse, for instance, means that some sensitive political topics are no longer forbidden but function to provide timely nationalist narratives. In particular, these narratives politicize, nationalize and stimulate an online consumer culture with the dual purpose of encouraging personal freedoms, but also a common consumer identity. The Chinese government's shrewd strategy thus minimizes the need for direct political and/or policing intervention by simultaneously and indirectly controlling the self-managing consumers it champions.

Foucault's concept of governmentality

Since Foucault's theorization of governmentality uniquely explicates the sort of complex governance strategies the CCP employs, I chose it is as the theoretical framework for the analysis in this book. French historian and philosopher Michel Foucault was one of the most influential thinkers of the twentieth century. His wide-ranging examinations of the uses of power, discourse, language and politics are used extensively in many disciplines. His concern to reveal power relations and the subjectivities they involve people in is evident in all his work, for instance in his groundbreaking studies of sexuality (1984) just before his death and his studies of the organizational lives of institutions such as schools, prisons (e.g., 1977), clinics (e.g., 1973) and army barracks. Foucault's essays on the subject of government were published in *The Foucault effect: Studies in governmentality* (Burchell, Gordon & Miller 1991), a collection that deals with how specific government activities are conceived and arranged (Dean 2002, p. 37; Rose & Miller 1992, p. 181). Together, the essays examine the thought behind the activity of government, make Foucault's ideas more accessible (Gordon 1991, p. 1), and have opened the way for further consideration of Foucault's conception of governmentality.

The use of Foucault's governmentality in this book is not a simple uptake of these essays; the analysis applies the Foucauldian theory in a critical manner. On one hand, I use Foucault's conception of governmentality to explain the tactics of governmentality in China. On the other hand, examining governmentality at work in Chinese society can display the liberal use of governmentality in non-liberal countries, which is not covered in this theory. In fact, this research could demonstrate the liberal practice of governmentality in the Chinese context to enrich the understanding of governmentality in the Western context.

Foucault's theorization of governmentality provided a new understanding of power as a way of doing things, whereby, for instance, sovereignty and discipline in nation-states which subject individuals to the codes and practices of an authoritarian regime could be understood as practical (see Burchell, Gordon & Miller 1991). Although most theorists treat government as a methodical and rational task, one which can be positioned as liberal or illiberal (e.g., Burchell 1996, p. 19), for Foucault, at least, government signified much more than centre-state politics; it implied a wide range of entities that could be controlled implicitly and indirectly as well as by direct rule.

Governmentality addresses how the people who govern and the people who are governed are conceived as well as how rulers govern and subjects are governed. In short, analyses of governmentality address "the conduct of conduct" (Dean 1999, p. 10). The hybrid term "govern-mentality" combines the ideologies and actions of government and how these are communicated and received among the governed. Thus it also includes discourse. Foucault himself explains the role of discourse in governance as follows:

> In a society such as ours, but basically in any society, there are manifold relations of power which permeate, characterize and constitute the social body, and these relations of power cannot themselves be established, consolidated nor implemented without the production, accumulation, circulation and functioning of a discourse. There can be no possible exercise of power without a certain economy of discourse of truth which operates through and on the basis of this association. We are subjected to the production of truth through power and we cannot exercise power except through the production of truth. (1991, p. 93)

His explanation offers a complex account of the relations between power and its promulgation. People are persuaded to comply with a government by the ways in which those governing manufacture truths. Foucault was, therefore, essentially interested in the technologies of governance, which include the various means by which power is decentralized but maintained through being made unquestionable, bearable or palatable. Accordingly, this study seeks to make sense of some of the generally unquestioned practices (see Dean 1999, p. 16) of Chinese governance.

Foucault situates the concept of governmentality in Western notions of freedom and liberalism (Sigley 2006), and researchers who have since added to Foucault's insights, making them more concrete (Aitken 2007), have continued to make Western nation-states their primary sites of analysis. Indeed, applying a governmentality frame to China may initially appear inappropriate.

The gulf between liberal forms of governmentality and China is more apparent than real, however. Liberal and non-liberal societies are related as two sides of a coin are related, because conceptualizing liberalism is largely reliant on being able to conceptualize its opposite, an illiberal other (Stokes 1959). In non-liberal countries such as China, one needs to remember that

> [a]lthough Maoist socialism, for example, may seem as far removed from systems of Western liberalism as one can imagine, all "modern" systems of government are cut from the same cloth. (Sigley 2006, p. 491)

Foucault (1991) states that in older forms of government, liberalism does not replace sovereignty and discipline but merges with them. In reality, theoretically liberal democratic governments today can be quite "unfree" (Hindess, 2001a). Hindess goes on to argue that sovereign and authoritarian measures, in fact, constructively influence the development of liberal attitudes and behaviours (2001a & b). It would seem, then, that in effect understanding liberalism relies upon the theorization of restraint. A liberal government with non-liberal features does not deny liberal principles; instead, liberal and non-liberal features are mutually dependent.

Thus, while theorists such as Hindess (2001a) and Dean (2002) primarily examine liberal conceptions of government in the West, they have also broached the issue of how governmentality operates in other settings. In practice, non-liberal regimes and liberal governments are composed of similar political features — for example, balances of pastoral power and sovereignty — even though each nation-state's balance is clearly distinctive as liberal or non-liberal. But as first Dean (2002) and then Sigley (2006) note, the ultimate difference between liberal and non-liberal governments is that the former enable, and encourage, citizens' experience of freedom and its continuing improvement. For example, a society in which some members are judged ready for self-regulation and others are not, the latter at least have the prospect of future freedom and self-regulation (Dean 2002; Hindess 2001a & b). Non-liberal regimes, by contrast, do not (Dean 1999, p. 147).

In the end, however, what both types of governments assume and hold in common may be more important than the beliefs or activities that separate them (Hindess 1996). The recent example of the Chinese government's encouragement of individual consumerism and the personal pursuit of pleasure is a significant case in point, and it makes China's strategies of governance particularly interesting. Since research to date has shown that the boundaries between liberal and non-liberal forms of government are blurred, this narrows the gulf between Western liberalism and the Chinese context considerably.

Clearly, however, there is still room for further investigation. Since the turn of the century, a number of studies in non-Western instances of governmentality have been conducted, some of them on China. One study has examined how the government handles prostitution businesses and practices in China (Jeffrey 2004). A wide-ranging study has explored major changes of governance in contemporary China and their significance for a non-democratic regime (Sigley 2006). Another has focused on Chinese governance and the ageing population (Powell 2000). Yet another has examined the concepts of choice and autonomy emerging in current China (Hoffman 2006). Even more recently, a critique of Maoism and its implications has argued the existence of revolutionary governmentality, a "type of politics that the Western liberal political science fails to recognize" (Dutton 2008, p. 11). Apart from anything else, the range and diversity of such studies demonstrate the potential of the concept of governmentality as a theoretical frame for critiquing China's potential for political reform.

The method of critique

The focus of this book opens up an interdisciplinary dialogue between cultural studies and Internet studies. The study's theoretical reorientation of Internet studies to encompass not only empirical research but also the reality of China's socio-cultural context is particularly important. It is impossible to understand how China will manage its own political future, including the development of its own version of cyberspace, unless research on Chinese Internet usage and its role in democratization takes into account the underlying socio-political reasons for it and how it is generally used.

In assessing China's immediate potential for development as a democracy, this book examines the recent central case of Chinese bloggers' anger using the themes of censorship and nationalism within the macro-theme or framework of governmentality. These conceptual themes frame the discussions in each chapter. The book concludes that the structural changes required for political democratization in China are unlikely in the foreseeable future despite increasing cyberspace activity among Chinese people.

The sources and methods employed in this book are mainly qualitative although quantitative analysis contributed to Chapter 2, Consumer Liberalism. This chapter, involving a case study of Chinese blogging practices and their political implications, thematically analyses selected texts and discourse, and contexts of Chinese cyberspace usage, but it also includes quantitative typologies and statistics. The turnover rate of blogs and the deletion of files posed a serious challenge. My research design was influenced by the procedures recently used by other researchers in similar studies. In a study of Chinese Blog Service Providers (BSPs) in early 2009 on censorship practices, MacKinnon used a seven-step strategy:

1. Log into the blog of one BSP, copy and paste the content unit into the "back end" edit window of the blog; take a screenshot;

2. Hit "publish." If the content is blocked from publication, or "held for moderation" take a screenshot of what kind of error message or other message appeared;

3. If the content is not blocked from publication, take a screenshot of what the blog post looks like when the author is logged into the system;

4. Log out and check whether the content is still visible to the public, not just the logged-in author. Take a screenshot;

5. Check back 24-48 hours later to see if the blog post is still visible. Take a screenshot showing either the still visible post, or the error message saying "this page does not exist," or whatever else can be seen;

6. Access the blog post on a mainland Chinese ISP to see whether it is accessible (*i.e.,* not filtered) on at least one Chinese domestic ISP. Take a screenshot;

7. Upload all of these screenshots into a database according to the unique number assigned to the content unit, along with descriptive comments noting any interesting or unusual circumstances surrounding the situations in which censorship occurred. (MacKinnon 2009a)

I customized a three-step method based on MacKinnon's seven steps:

1. Log into one BSP, type the "sensitive keywords" into its search engine, hit "search".

2. Take a screenshot of the search results.

3. Upload all these screenshots into a database according to the same keywords.

Organization of the book

The book has three parts. Part I introduces the focus and argument (this chapter) and examines the catalyst (Chapter 2) for the research in a case study of Chinese bloggers' anger at the West's criticisms of the Chinese government's restrictions of people's independent Internet usage to online consumerism.

Part II problematizes the anger. Chapter 3 provides a historical context for Chinese Generation Y's nationalism and support for the Chinese central government, demonstrating why this young generation is as content as the Chinese government with the current degrees of personal freedom. Chapter 4 examines Chinese Generation Y's national fervour from another angle, strengthening the argument for this generation's general contentment with the political regime. Due to the current, unprecedented freedoms of speech and action, present personal liberties are greatly appreciated, negating the need for further structural changes on the part of the CCP. Chapter 5 examines the Western media's attention to Chinese censorship, critiquing its expectations of unrest and calls for political reforms to follow online censorship, based on Western experience of democratic movements.

Chapter 6, which opens Part III, elucidates the role of the Chinese government in forestalling political unrest through its subtle management of Chinese bloggers' national loyalty via a case study of the Anti-CNN web-community. The personal empowerment Chinese netizens have experienced online as consumers and contributors to debates on matters of national importance provides the basis for the argument in the final chapter, Chapter 7, that, compared with previous generations, Chinese Internet users enjoy many economic and political freedoms. So the political reforms Western commentators have been anticipating are extremely unlikely to occur in the immediate future.

2

二

Consumer Liberalism

The individual as consumer

Interest in buying and personal pleasure is the most common feature of Chinese blogging. Ideologically, this has been called "consumerism as economic individualism". Chinese bloggers are self-managing consumers rather than free citizens. Their embrace of consumer values is a striking feature of China's cyberspace. The Chinese blogosphere contains relatively few political blogs compared with the mainstream blogs, which feature individual pursuits and the purchase of material goods.

The five key characteristics of the Chinese blogging community that emerge from the case study analysis and which this chapter critiques are:

1. Individualist and consumerist ideologies can be distinguished in the majority of Chinese bloggers' writings.

2. Although political blogs do exist in China's blogosphere, they are mainly part of the nationalistic narrative.

3. Blogs expressing political dissent exist in China's blogosphere, but the readership is rather small.

4. Political-satire blogs criticizing the government have a relatively large numbers of readers, but their interest-value is entertainment.

5. Censorship is mainly self-implemented, that is, enforcing mechanisms are rarely needed.

Statistical and thematic analyses of the Chinese blogging community in this chapter comprise the case study that supports these statements. First, however, I offer some contextual background for these analyses.

The sudden availability of free, personal space, which was not available in previous decades, ignited a passion for blogging in China. In comparison with chatting, gaming, or reading news online, more and more Chinese now choose to write blogs to express their emotions, record their ordinary life; and more and more bloggers have found the joy of "living online". Good-looking homepages, brilliant comments and messages from strangers, all have brought bloggers extensive enjoyment. Large numbers of readers have made many grass-root bloggers famous. As a Chinese scholar observes, blogging in China has flourished owing to the variety of benefits it has brought to many people (Xiaolisishen, 2007). Celebrities are blogging for fame, businessmen are blogging for profit, and general bloggers are blogging for emotional fulfillment and to express attitudes or opinions. The consequent personal freedom has enabled Chinese bloggers to become self-managing consumers who experience a degree of independence which, at the same time, legitimates and stabilizes the existing political framework — hence the increasing interest in the role of the Chinese blogging community in current development in China.

Why is consumerism as economic individualism the most prevalent ideology enacted in Chinese cyberspace nowadays?

The embracing of consumerism

Being a consumer is currently highly prized among Chinese blogosphere users. Consequently, Chinese Internet companies, as a Morgan Stanley analysis (2005) indicated, are encouraging this respect and interest to its utmost. The report argues that

> … Chinese Internet companies that focus on creating consumer value have the highest potential to create shareholder value. China is No. 1 in the world in mobile subscribers and No. 1 in Internet users under the age of 30 — this evolving presence on the world stage should not be underestimated. (Morgan Stanley Report 2005, p. 1)

A decade ago, Ma concluded that China's media landscape displayed "uneven liberalization" in its range of apolitical and political content (Ma 2000, p. 21). This imbalance is still strongly evident in China's cyberspace: bloggers of apolitical materials enjoy a high degree of autonomy in Chinese cyberspace, and although political content is posted more often and more visibly than previously, it is available only within the contexts of consumerist discourse. Moreover, the Chinese state is policing the Internet through sophisticated controlling strategies, which endorse consumerism rather than political thought. Although new kinds of media use in China such as blogging actually create cultural values, Yu (2007) believes that online users do

> not challenge the mainstream culture (be it political or business), but rather deconstruct it through playful (mis)use (and often juxtaposition) of the available resources. (p. 429)

Chinese netizens are actually pursuing entertainment for entertainment's sake. Assuming that Yu is correct, Chinese people's empowerment through participation in Chinese cyberspace for whatever purposes — be they political or market-oriented — is ultimately entangled with a consumerist ideology.

This position is corroborated by a series of survey reports on Internet use in China between 2007 and 2009:

- the China Internet Network Information Centre (CNNIC)'s *19th, 21st and 23rd Statistical Survey Reports on the Internet Development in China* (released, January 2007, 2008, and 2009 respectively, hereafter referred to as the CNNIC 19th, 21st and 23rd Surveys)
- Morgan Stanley's *The China Internet Report* published in 2005 (hereafter referred to as the Morgan Stanley Report 2005)
- a comparative survey conducted by Norton from Symantec on online habits in twelve countries (referred to as the Norton Online Living Report 2009).

According to these reports, reading online news, chatting online, searching for information, sending and receiving e-mails and playing online games are popular activities among Chinese Internet users. Although different organizations under different circumstances collected the data, the results are remarkably consistent. The statistics in both the CNNIC surveys (viewed 7 March 2009, online) and the Morgan Stanley Report demonstrate a consumer-oriented culture in Chinese cyberspace. The Morgan Stanley report indicates three factors instrumental in bringing about the cultural evolution Chinese consumers have long been craving: free-floating information, interactivity and entertainment (Morgan Stanley report 2005, p. 5). The CNNIC surveys provide a more detailed analysis of Chinese netizens' online activities, identifying eight categories of usage: reading news, searching for information, communication (chatting and e-mail), social-networking (making friends through websites and blogging), entertainment (online gaming, listening to music and watching videos), e-business, e-banking and e-education.

The cultural diffusion of consumerism is a familiar, worldwide phenomenon (Qiu 2003). However, Chinese netizens' embrace of consumerism is astonishing. The Norton Online Living Report (2009), which surveyed nearly 9,000 adults and children in 12 countries (the US, Canada, the UK, France, Germany, Italy, Sweden, Japan, India, Australia and Brazil, as well as China) on their online habits, asked participants whether they used the Internet for more than an hour a month. This survey, the most recent comparative study of global Internet use at the time of writing, discovered that consumer use largely reflects how people value Internet resources and that people in different countries — such as China and the US, which have the largest online populations — act very differently, reflecting different cultural preferences. According to the survey, the Chinese in general are more likely than Americans to embrace new technologies. Eighty-two per cent of Chinese Internet users surveyed visit social-networking sites, compared with just 47 per cent in the US; 54 per cent of Chinese respondents play online games frequently or constantly compared with 27 per cent in the US, and; 56 per cent of Chinese people surveyed spend at least 10 hours per month online, more than nine times the 6 per cent who go online in the US.

The consumer culture in Chinese cyberspace is astonishing but understandable when considered in the context of changing China. China is an enormous country, once handicapped by poverty and Communist ideology, but now flooded with consumerist ideology. An iPod Nano costs US$179.84 in China, which is more than an average person's monthly pay, but there are still plenty of white earphones on show in the country (French 2007). For those Chinese whose monthly pay is around US$1000, spending 80 per cent of their salary on a Louis Vuitton key ring is not unusual (QQ News 2008). Cases of showing off luxury shopping and richness in one's blog are plentiful (Netease News 2008).

Consumerism is not a Chinese word, and what is special about China is the totally opposite ideology that existed before its appearance in China. The country and its people shifted from being willing to endure hardship in the 1970s and 1980s to seeking pleasure (Qiu 2003). Most recently, then, hedonism has transformed Chinese citizens into enthusiastic online consumers. The transition came about as follows.

In 1949, the Communist party led by Mao Zedong established the People's Republic of China. The new government, founded by the Communist Party and guided by Marxist-Leninist-Maoist ideology, dominated the country (Lawrence 1998). The Mao government nationalized private enterprise, subtly controlling the population's everyday lives by regimenting their daily activities in the name of socialist reconstruction. Thus, the new China established by Mao became one of the most extreme examples of state-controlled ideology, education, and individual expression.

Following the succession of Deng Xiaoping in 1978, the country shifted focus to market-based, economic development. In the early 1990s, following Deng Xiaoping's trip to southern China and his call on the nation to move ahead faster with economic reforms, China started to witness its extraordinary economic boom (Hamrin & Zhao 1995). Deng pronounced an era of "reform and opening up" in 1995. This move led to dramatic changes not only in the economy, but also in society, focusing in particular on relations between town and country, thus opening up the whole country to the outside world. Specific developments included a reduction of rural poverty, an increase in migration between rural and urban areas and improvements in urban living conditions through, for example, a transition from state provision of urban housing to more private home ownership over a 15-year period (Wang 2004, p. 148). In these ways, many Chinese experienced freedom that would have previously been unthinkable: they were able to move around the country, choose their own jobs, earn more money, and purchase commodities that could not have been imagined before (Hamrin & Zhao 1995).

Once it was possible for sections of the population to earn more money than before, the pursuit of "getting rich first" before any other life-goals began and very quickly progressed at an astonishing speed. This phenomenon is corroborated by Hewitt (2007), who, based on his own recent experience of living in China, argues that getting rich has indeed become the prerequisite for most Chinese nowadays. The disposable incomes of families and individuals in urban and even some rural areas have enabled more and more Chinese to embrace consumerism and realize their monetary goals. Both the speed and the extent of the spread of consumerism in China are unprecedented. Consumerism has spread not only throughout big cities like Beijing and Shanghai but has also reached county-level cities. Although consumerism in large metropolises is to be expected (see Gerth 2003; Hewitt 2007), it can be slow to take hold of more isolated cities. Yet I witnessed such growth of consumer interest myself in 2008.

On 28 December 2008, I went to a county-level city in China where my grandparents were born. It is located in the middle of Jiangsu Province in the Yangtze Delta region of China. This city is underdeveloped in comparison with many other cities in China. On this day, a ceremony was held to mark the opening of a new shopping mall in that city, and hundreds and thousands of local residents were squashed in front of the gate at the entrance to the mall, struggling to be the first to get in when the gates opened. The shopping mall in this Chinese city, a smaller and simpler version of the Wangfujing in Beijing or the New Street Plaza in Nanjing, is a visual symbol of what has become known as China's "consumer revolution" (Li 1998; Wu 1998; Davis 2000). Amid the advertisements outside the shopping mall, a poster stated "Protect consumer rights" in bold writing. The out-of-date poster design in this developing city might appear less cosmopolitan than those displayed in cities such as Beijing or Shanghai, but it reflects an aspect of China's consumer revolution that has been spreading to smaller cities throughout the country. Namely, the promotion of personal values and consumer rights has reached the county-level and is transforming Chinese citizens into consumers across the country. The analysis of a Chinese blogging community will illustrate this even more thoroughly.

The case of a Chinese blogging community

Statistical analysis

To compose the statistical figures for this case study, I collated and analyzed data from the CNNIC's own surveys. The CNNIC is a non-profit organization founded in June 1997 as the state's network information centre of China. The authority and objectivity of CNNIC's statistical survey reports are widely recognized by domestic and international scholars, for example, Christopher Hughes and Gudrun Wacker in *China and the Internet: the Great Leap Forward* (2003); Castells Manuel in *The Netword Society: a Cross-cultural Perspective* (2004); Jens Damm and Simona Thomas in *Chinese Cyberspaces: Technological Changes and Political Effects* (2006); Zixue Tai in *The Internet in China: Cyberspace and Civil Society* (2006); Yongming Zhou in *Historicizing Online Politics: Telegraphy, the Internet, and Political Participation in China* (2006), and; Yongnian Zheng in *Technological Empowerment* (2008). Hence, the technical data from CNNIC is, I suggest, trustworthy.

Blog contents

In the US, blogs with political content rank first, with news and political blogs holding the largest audience share at 43 per cent (Kerner 2005). In countries such as Australia and Canada, the number of political blogs written by independent commentators is increasing fast. Political ideas are already widely blogged in Malaysia, Pakistan and Sri Lanka. In contrast, in the Chinese blogosphere most Chinese bloggers focus on personal thoughts and entertainment-related activities (see Figure 2.1).

As Figure 2.1 indicates, 84.9 per cent of the blogs are monologues or records of the writers' emotions on their own conduct and status; blogs in China increasingly demonstrate these forms of the young generation's self-absorption.

Age Composition

More than 70 per cent of Chinese bloggers are under 30 years old (see Figure 2.2). The age composition of Chinese bloggers is a crucial factor in the apolitical blogosphere in China. Most Chinese bloggers were born after the 1980s and are members of China's Generation Y. The majority of these young bloggers in China use blogs as tools to record their personal thoughts.

Educational background

Nearly 70 per cent of Chinese bloggers have attended college or university (see Figure 2.3). The majority are young people who have had better opportunities than their parents did to go to university due to the changing education system in China from the late 1990s. Before then, China's higher education was reserved for certain elites (Elegant 2007). Those born after the 1980s who have benefited from the opening up of tertiary education appear proud of what the Chinese government has achieved and, not surprisingly, very positive about the government which has encouraged this expansion in education and the overall rising prosperity of China. Thus, the age composition of Chinese bloggers is consistent with the combination of a young Chinese blogger population and the blogosphere's mainstream apolitical content.

Bloggers and non-bloggers

To become a blogger, there are some prerequisites: regular access to the Internet, basic Internet knowledge, motivation and enough time. The number of Chinese bloggers has grown sharply but juxtaposing the blogger community against the wider population of China reveals that blogging as a vehicle for self-presentation reaches only a small section of the population (see Figure 2.4).

Even though blogs are used for political participation in China, it is not likely that a vehicle used by only 10 per cent of the population as a whole will lead a nation to democracy — especially as so much blog content is apolitical. Although the number of bloggers in China has reached 162 million, note that this is still only about 10 per cent of the total population.

In a money-oriented society in which consumerism is promoted, Chinese bloggers go online seeking various but quite specific returns. The analysis that follows identifies ten themes (that is, preferred types of blogs) based on frequency of use.

Thematic analysis

The following categorizations reflect a content analysis of blog behaviour, which I combined with the results of the most comprehensive survey report available (for this, see Xiaolisishen 2007). I first investigated two main blog servers in China, Sina blogs and QQ blogs, both of which follow their own systems of blog categorization. I examined individual blogs on both sites and then assessed and compared the two servers' systems of categorization before finally merging my category analysis with that reported in Xiaolisishen (2007) and ranking the composite findings. The first four most popular blog categories by frequency of use in

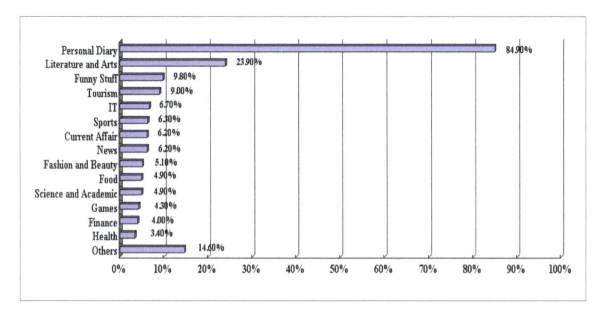

Figure 2.1: Statistical analysis of Chinese blogosphere: Contents
Source: Author's own compilation based on data from the CNNIC 2007, 2008, 2009

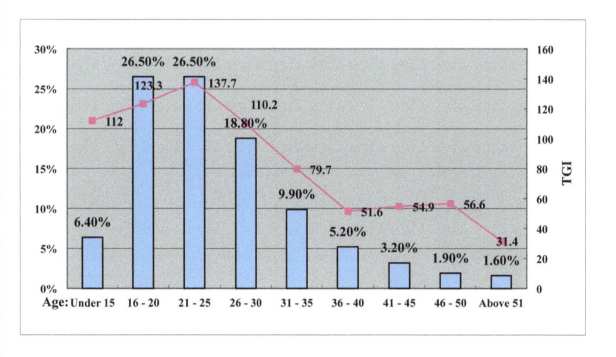

Figure 2.2: Statistical analysis of Chinese blogosphere: Age composition
Source: Author's own compilation based on data from CNNIC 2007, 2008, 2009

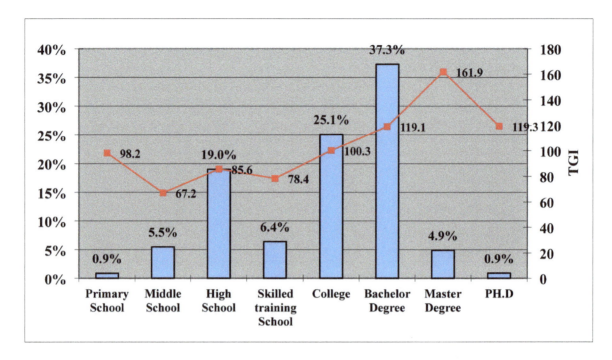

Figure 2.3: Statistical analysis of Chinese blogosphere: Educational background
Source: Author's own compilation based on data from CNNIC 2007, 2008, 2009

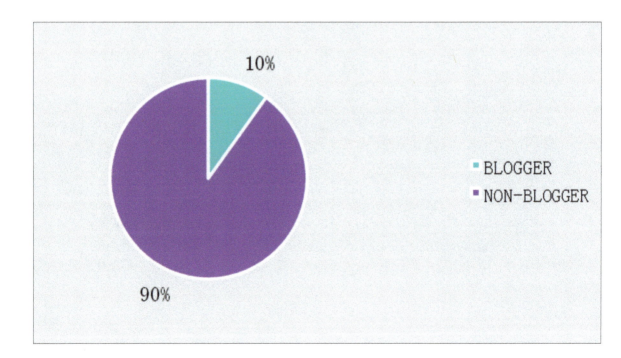

Figure 2.4: Statistical analysis of Chinese blogosphere: Bloggers and non-bloggers
Source: Author's own compilation based on data from CNNIC 2007, 2008, 2009

China appear first in the analysis. I then describe the remaining six categories, but only briefly. Categorization analyses of this kind, however, are always relative rather than *absolute*, so the categories featured below are not necessarily absolutely discrete.

Emotion [emo] blogs

I found that writing blogs to record one's emotions is one of the most popular types of blogging in China. Previously, many people favoured online gaming, music or movies. Nowadays writing blogs has become a more personal activity for self-entertainment. Pei Wang, 25, a young mum who lives in Nanjing, said on her blog:

> Turn on my computer in the morning, log on to my blog chronically, I am so used to it that it has become one of my habits, I have learnt how to live my life more meaningfully through writing blogs. … Blogging is the motivation of my life, I search every interesting story in my life for it, and it brings me unlimited joy in return. (Wang 2009)

Although writing blogs about her thoughts and feelings couldn't be expected to bring Pei any material benefits, the spiritual fortune and the happiness she evidently finds is more important for this kind of blogger than gaining any material possessions.

Net star blogs

The Chinese Internet has made a great deal of "Internet Hot Stars" nationally. For example, amongst many other hot grassroots bloggers, "February Girl" was brave enough to expose her body shape on her blog; "Shan Dong Top Brother" dared to propose to celebrity Xu Jing Lei, and; "Ai Qing Qing" used a pin as an exchange for more valuable things and eventually got a villa home in 100 days. These up-to-the-minute, trendy netizens gained nationwide attention and fame through their daring, bold actions.

Muzi Mei is a typical example here of a "hot star blogger", a young female journalist and blogger from Guangzhou who became a controversial household name in China in late 2003. Her real name is Li Li (李丽 *Li Li*); "Muzi" (木子) becomes "Li" (李) when the characters are stacked vertically, and "Mei" (美) and "Li" (丽) are both synonyms for "beautiful" (Wikipedia Contributors, 2008). Her blog, which posted detailed descriptions of her sexual encounters with men, was the first blog to breach the government's restrictions on sexual material and nudity. She became the media's hot topic across China in 2003, and the West soon covered her story (for example, *The New York Times* 2003; *The Telegraph* 2003). The Chinese government then circulated an official letter calling for such media coverage to end, after which the heated discussion of her blog cooled down. But blogging certainly brought her material benefits: she was hired by Bokee.com, the top Chinese blog service provider (BSP) as a marketing manager.

Celebrity blogs

More and more celebrities started blogs because of their potential commercial value. The rapid rise of blogs is thus also an effect of the cult of celebrity in China. Many celebrities from a range of backgrounds now blog, including movie stars Jackie Chen, Jet Lee and Xu Jing Lei;

famous singer GG Liang; super girls (Chinese idols) Li Yu Chun and He Jie; genius writers Han Han, Guo Jing Ming and Zhen Yuan Jie; business elites Niu Gen Sheng and Pan Shi Qi, and; sports star Guo Jing Jing. By blogging, celebrities cannot but attract their loyal fans and the media's attention. Blogs, therefore, have become the main source of entertainment news.

Xu Jinglei is an example of this phenomenon, an actress and director in Mainland China, who graduated from the prestigious Beijing Film Academy in 1997. Although not a celebrity abroad, Xu Jinglei is a household name across China. In mid 2006, her Chinese language blog in Sina "had the most incoming links of any blog in any language on the Internet" (Asian Truly 2009). According to Xu, blog writing is the "most convenient and economic way of publicizing her films" (Baiwai Online 2006); she has certainly been successful in using her blog as a platform for her new movies. For example, in 2006, she posted the details of the filming process and market plans of her movie *Dreams May Come*, and included links to clips from the film in her blog. China Mobile seized the opportunity and inserted a link at the top of her blog's homepage with an announcement that the theme song of *Dreams May Come* sung by Xu Jinlei was downloadable for ring-tone cell-phones (Baiwai Online 2006). Xu Jinglei recorded her 247-millionth blog-site hit in 2009 (Sinablog 2009). Unlike Muzi Mei, Xu gained fame by focusing on her work and ordinary life. Xu Jinglei was one of the first celebrities that started posting on Sinablog in 2005 (*The Guardian* 2007). Now Sina has around 3,000 celebrities blogging.

Beauty blogs

Pretty girls write blogs for a range of reasons. Beauty blogs, for example, are popular in the Chinese blogosphere. Examples of this type of blog include those of the beauty writer "Annie Baby", Internet talent girl "An Xiao Ying", and so-called bewitchingly beautiful woman "Baby Yi", as well as more generic categories such as "natural beauty", "bus beauty", and "fashion beauty". The bloggers' photos and writings attract a large number of readers, and some of the beauties have become famous. Blog portal Poboo started holding Blogger Babe competitions in 2006, in which both the beauty and the writing of blogging babes were evaluated by netizen judges (Poboo.cn 2006). During the competitions, more than 10,000 'pretty girls' registered their interests, more than 7 million netizens voted for the competitions, and more than 200,000 people logged on Poboo daily to follow the competitions.

Yi Lan, who was the winner of the first Blogger Babe Competition in 2006, is from northeast China. Although being a winner did not bring her significant direct benefits, she has become famous as a well-known beauty blogger.

Meeting friends and sexual partners through blogs

The Chinese blogosphere has become a place for making friends. Many bloggers have found their other half through blogging, while others are looking for a one-night-stand only. Generally speaking, since blog portals in China such as Sina, Bokee, and QQ have provided platform space for making friends, many young people have become involved. Blogging activities between the different blog groups that have sprung up have increased bloggers' opportunities to make new friends.

Advertisement blogs

Blogs with large numbers of visitors started posting advertisements one after the other. Although the advertisements market in the blogosphere is not as mature as on the major websites, it has great development potential because "Where is people, there is advertisement". Moreover, blogs would not survive in an advertisement-free atmosphere.

Magazine blogs

Many Chinese magazines such as Ming Shi magazine, Fashion Gentleman magazine, Chinese Entertainment Report, Chinese Hairdressing Fashion Report, and Movie Coverage are shifting their publications into the blogosphere. Editors find they are able to communicate with their readers more directly online, and as more and more readers are able to access the Internet they too appreciate its speed and efficiency, as well as the wide range of reading material now available online.

Specialty blogs

Yet other blogs in the Chinese blogosphere specialize in particular topics. From hairdressing and cooking, to stock markets and sexual knowledge, specialty blogs play an educational role.

Entertainment blogs

Because of the national interest in celebrity figures, entertainment gossip flourishes in China. It is widely understood that blogs that have more than one million visitors in China are either celebrity blogs or entertainment blogs. The high numbers of visitors generate potentially huge commercial value. For example, Andy, who does celebrities paintings on his entertainment blog in China, sells each of his drawings at prices based on their online demand (QQ Read 2008).

News blogs

With the expanding use and impact of blogging, the Chinese blogosphere has become an important birthplace of social news. Blogging has given people who were formerly only news consumers the right to write news. Chinese netizens are enjoying this previously-undreamed-of freedom, although it is limited to apolitical issues. Blogging service providers (BSPs) highlight different social issues — such as "the harelip event of Li Ya Peng's daughter", "Harmonious society recalls Lei Feng", "Who is controlling our house price?", "Is 'Lust and Caution' a good movie?", and issues arising from the Chinese super girl competition, a competition similar to American Idol — so the parameters they choose make them social newsmakers too.

The case for political freedom in the Chinese blogosphere

In the Chinese blogosphere, as already noted, there are relatively few political blogs compared with the mainstream blogs that feature individualism and consumerism. Political blogs are a very small portion of the whole and blogs posted demonstrate that readers' primary interests are in entertainment. I will illustrate their preferences for individualism and consumerism through the promotional efforts of three leading blog service providers: Sina Blog, Blogbus, and QZone.

Firstly, among all the blog categories Sina Blog offers, the only category that fits in the political genre explicitly is "military affairs" blogs (see Figure 2.5); in the case of Blogbus and QZone there are no explicitly political categories (see respectively Figures 2.6 and 2.7).

Although most Chinese BSPs do not provide an explicit politics category, political blogs can be found posted with other name tags such as "law forum" or "law hotline" (see Figure 2.8).

Based on the list of sensitive topics found — most sources (for example, Wikipedia, *Washington Post, China Digital Times*) claim these are filtered — the types of political blogs can be categorized in four groups: political blogs with non-sensitive material, political blogs with sensitive material, political satire blogs, and political blogs with explicit anti-government material. This type of typological analysis can only be relative, as I have already mentioned, but it does reveal representative examples that, interestingly, display a variety of other phenomena as well, sometimes all going on in one single blog.

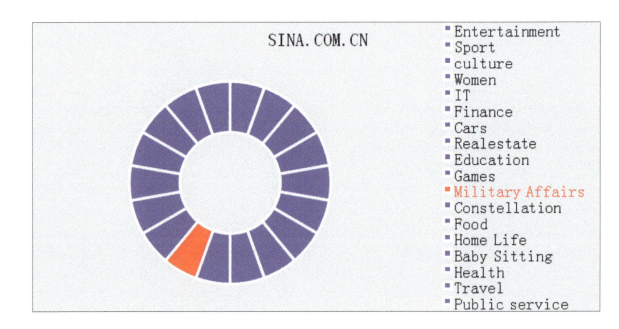

Figure 2.5: Categories of Sina Blog
Source: Author's own compilation based on data from Sina Blog 2009

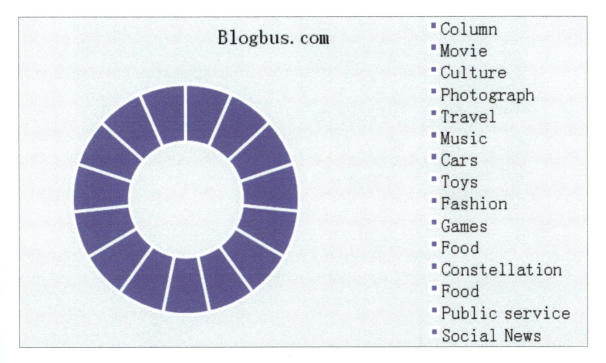

Figure 2.6: Categories of Blogbus
Source: Author's own compilation based on data from Blogbus 2009

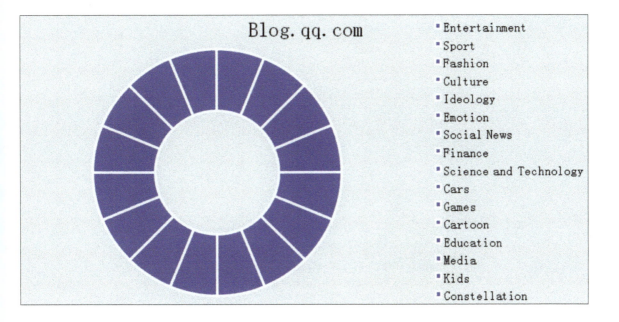

Figure 2.7: Categories of QQ Blog
Source: Author's own compilation based on data from QQ Blog 2009

Figure 2.8: Example of government official blogs: News office of Tangshan City Council
Source: http://blog.sina.com.cn/tangshanren2008

Figure 2.9: Examples of participatory blogs contain no explicitly sensitive topics in Chinese cyberspace
Source: http://blog.sina.com.cn/way45320

Figure 2.10: Examples of participatory blogs contain no explicitly sensitive topics in Chinese cyberspace
Source: http://blog.163.com

Figure 2.11: Examples of participatory blogs contain no explicitly sensitive topics in Chinese cyberspace
Source: http://blog.focus.cn

Keywords	Google Blog	Sina Blog	Blogbus	QQzone
民主 democracy	3,295,563	6,127,266	2442	695
人权 human rights	942,224	0	1223	114
独裁 dictatorship	701,417	0	292	0
反党 anti-Party	61,444	113610	9	340
反革命 Counterrevolutionary	227,268	437316	2442	695
红色恐怖 red-terror	9,197	0	2	11748 (INVALID)
种族灭绝 genocide	32,488	93480	14	518
镇压 oppression	443,923	0	149	12
反共 anti-Communist	73,104	0	17	0
共匪 Communist-bandits	0	0	3	135
六四 4th June	0	0	NA	0
天安门事件 Tiananmen Square massacre	0	0	3	23 (INVALID)
民运 Chinese democracy movement	0	0	71	0
文革 Cultural Revolution	1,144,707	0	466	0
王丹 Wang Dan	35,378	0	NA	296 (INVALID)
魏京生 Wei Jingsheng	0	0	NA	46 (INVALID)
吾尔开希 Wu'er Kaixi	0	0	NA	0
柴玲 Chai Ling	2,063	0	NA	0
封从德 Feng Congde	379	28	NA	5 (INVALID)
天安门母亲 Tiananmen Mothers	1,172	0	NA	50 (INVALID)
刘宾雁 Liu Binyan	3,886	0	NA	4 (INVALID)
一塌糊涂 YTHT BBS	1,515	677	NA	111
汕尾 Shanwei	97320(INVALID)	0	na	240 (INVALID)
疆独 Xinjiang independence	29,131	0	na	3001 (INVALID)
藏独 Tibetan independence	465,259	0	na	424
流亡政府 Exile	27,338	169854	19	39
达赖 *Dalai*	344, 912	0	293	0
西藏论坛 Tibet Talk	16	34	na	16 (INVALID)
方舟子 Fang Zhouzi	43147	104820	na	133
江泽民 Jiang Zemin	0	0	na	0
赵紫阳 Zhao Ziyang	0	0	na	401
大纪元 Epoch	0	0	na	0
自由亚洲 Free Asia	11, 443	921	na	461
美国之音 Voice of America	125, 203	0	na	6 (INVALID)
台独 Taiwan independence	350, 900	0	114	250
九评共产党 The Nine Commentaries on the Communist Party	0	0	8	0
媒体审查 Media censorship	346	118	0	2816 (INVALID)
网络审查 Internet censorship	177, 667	389	na	11116
李洪志 Li hongzhi	0	0	3	0
丁子霖 Ding Zilin	1, 691	0	na	28 (INVALID)
吴弘达 Harry Wu	369	31	na	5 (INVALID)
王若望 Wang Ruowang	1, 212	190	na	35(INVALID)

Figure 2.12: Statistics on political blogs with sensitive materials in China
Source: Author's own compilation based on statistical analysis

Political blogs with non-sensitive materials

Political blogs with non-sensitive keywords are of two main types: government official blogs and political, participatory blogs by grassroots agencies. From central to provincial and municipal to village levels, Chinese party agencies have started blogging. However, these official blogs are normally non-active. For example, a blog set up by the news office of Tangshan City Council on 22 May 2008 was active for no longer than one day. It has only six blog entries and stopped posting new entries on the 23 May 2008 (see Figure 2.9).

By contrast, there are politically oriented blogs that allow participation although they contain no explicitly sensitive topics. From bloggers named "a nobody criticizes the government", "joking about current affairs" and "looking at current affairs" (see Figures 2.10 and 2.11), Chinese bloggers seem to have the freedom to discuss government policies and comment on current affairs in their blogs — but in reality, the comments are not critical.

Political blogs with sensitive materials

No similar statistical analysis of blogs with sensitive contents has been done in China, or elsewhere as far as I have discovered. Through this analysis, I found that blog entries with sensitive topics were hidden in mainstream consumerist and individual blogs. The methodology I employed to reach this conclusion was to search for keywords via each BSP's contents search-engine. This kind of analysis demanded advanced skill levels in Chinese reading and up-to-date knowledge of China's political and social situation. There was no reliable way to automate such an investigation, which ultimately depends upon individual interpretation at a given time.

There are more than 15 commercial BSPs catering to mainland Chinese bloggers. After considering the credibility and the manageability of the statistics, I chose Google blog search and 3 leading BSPs with thousands of Chinese blogs: Blogbus, QZone, and Sina. I picked out 50 topics generally considered sensitive by Western sources, which claim these topics are normally filtered in China (for example, Wikipedia, *Washington Post*, Open Net Initiative). I typed each topic into each BSP search-engine and took a screenshot of each result after searching. I then made sure each result was valid because in cases when no results of the keywords I typed in were found, the search-engine automatically directed me to the results of similar keywords. For example, when I searched "hong se kong bu" (red terror) in the search-engine of QZone, it displayed 11,748 results, a result of the engine searching "red" and "terror" separately. So these results referred to totally different things. This problem remained even when using Boolean search operators "red" and "terror" to help. In such cases, I considered the results invalid. Among the valid results, I also randomly checked whether full texts of the searched-for blog posts were visible to the public, then uploaded all of these screenshots into a database according to each keyword.

The analysis discovered that some blogs with sensitive materials do exist in the Chinese blogosphere: for example, the keyword "democracy" had more than three million results, "Cultural Revolution" had more than one million results, and "anti-Communist" had more than seventy thousand results (see Figure 2.12).

However, blogs with sensitive materials are mainly pro-China and adopt a nationalistic tone. For example, a blog entry containing the sensitive words "Tibetan separatists" had 135,075 readers, but the context condemned the Tibetan separatist who attacked the Chinese Olympic Torch holder Jin Jing in Paris. As the blog entry states, "Finally we found the stupid idiot who attacked the Olympic Torch holder 'Jin Jing', we should remember this stupid idiot, condemn him together, let him die with no burial place" (see Figure 2.13).

Blogs with dissenting materials

I also located blogs containing dissenting materials in the Chinese blogosphere. However, the readership appeared to be very small. For example, one blog condemned the Chinese Communist Party as a "bandit". It stated: "I started hating communist bandits in 1999, this is a capitalist world, but communist bandit enslaved us by textbooks and lied to us they would bring us good life". This blog entry, however, had only 14 readers (see Figure 2.14).

According to my research, then, although there are signs of political liberalism in China's cyberspace, they are only limited, and they do not form real grounds for arguing that political liberalism will take hold in the near future or that political democratization is already occurring in China's cyberspace. The limited personal and political freedom Chinese people now have is self-regulated; that is, there are no obvious signs of state censorship. The political equilibrium in Chinese cyberspace functions through what Foucault terms "technologies of the self" (1988a). These function also to legitimate and stabilize the existing political framework.

Political satire blogs

Political satire blogs are another category of Chinese political blogs. In these blogs, sensitive terms are transformed into Internet slang, and criticisms of current political leadership are narrated jokingly. The three most famous Internet slang expressions produced by these blogs are "river crab", "wearing three watches" and "grass mud horse".

"River crab" refers to Internet censorship in current China. The word "river crab" sounds similar to the word "harmonious" in Chinese Mandarin. Since building a harmonious society is the current Chinese government's goal, political activists describe the action of "being censored" as "being harmonized", hence "being river crabbed". "Wearing three watches" refers to "Three Represents", a political slogan coined by former President Jiang Zemin because "watch" and "represent" are homonymous in the Chinese language. "Grass mud horse" refers to a homonym for a well-known vulgarity in Chinese language: "cao ni mao" which means "Fuck your mother". Both the phrase "Fuck your mother" and word for

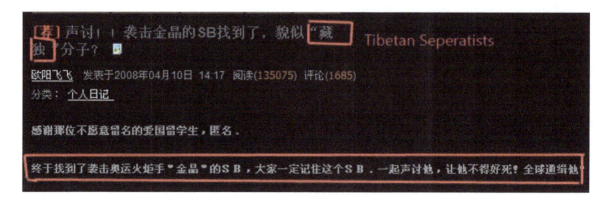

Figure 2.13: Example of political blogs with sensitive topic but in a nationalist tone
Source: http://user.qzone.qq.com/563172992/blog/1207808275 (accessed 17 June 2009)

过去的日子

<u>263963963</u>　发表于2008年02月26日　18:54　阅读(14) 评论(0)

分类：　<u>石頭記</u>

1998年，那年的冬天特别冷。

1999年春节。

我15岁，弟弟14岁。

我便是那时恨上匪共的。

因为这明明是一个资产阶级的世界　匪共却用教科书奴化了我们并跟我们说有好日子！

Figure 2.14: Example of dissent blogs
Source: http://user.qzone.qq.com/263963963/blog/1204023268 (accessed 13 June 2009)

Figure 2.15: River crab wearing three watches and grass mud horse
Source: http://chinadigitaltimes.net/china/grass-mud-horse/ (accessed 20 June 2009)

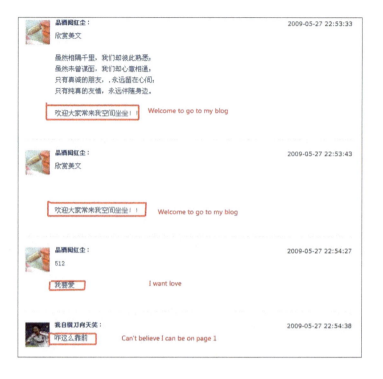

Figure 2.16: Samples of comments on Lee Cheng Peng's blog

horse are pronounced as "cao ni ma". In Chinese cyberspace, the phrase "grass mud horse" indicates the struggle against the evil "river crab" who "wears three watches", as the image in Figure 2.15 illustrates.

But it is important to notice two things: first, in comparison with the mainstream individualist and consumerist blogs, political satire blogs comprise a very small proportion of the whole. Second, although the readership of political satire blogs is much bigger than of blogs with dissenting materials, comments left by readers demonstrate distinctly what Yu (2007) argues, namely, blogs are predominantly entertainment for the sake of entertainment. For these reasons, political satire blogs are more accurately classified as entertainment than political. Moreover, in some cases, they are satirizing for material gain.

Take, for example, Lee Cheng Peng, who is one of the most popular satire bloggers in Sina Blogs. Although his satiric blogs have a relatively large number of visitors, most of their comments are not intended to be taken seriously. Lee Cheng Peng himself is using a satirical style to attract visitors and, hence, to sell his books. In one of the blog entries that jokes about the "grass mud horse", the number of readers is 121,099 and the number of comments posted is 1,216. While this disparity displays the popularity of this blogger and his style of writing, it also confirms that readers are pursuing entertainment rather than political information or debate, as the samples in Figure 2.16 show.

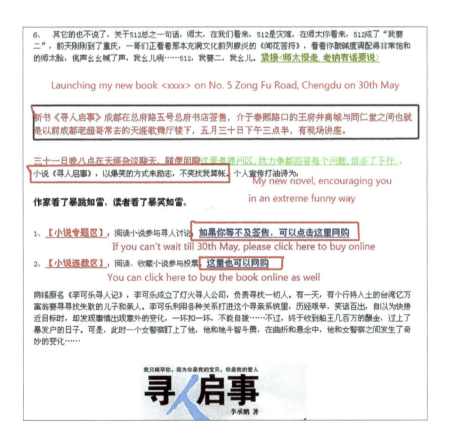

Figure 2.17: The benefits of Lee Cheng Peng's political satire blog
Source: http://blog.sina.com.cn/s/blog_46e7ba410100dao6.html#comment1 (accessed 23 June 2009)

The benefits Lee Cheng Peng's popular political satire blogs were bringing him are quite obvious. At the end of the body of the blog entry, he posted eye-catching announcements about selling his new book, using a different font, print size and colour and including the offer: "If you can't wait, please click here to buy my book online now" (see Figure 2.17).

Thus, use of the four types of political blogs examined shows that netizens are primarily interested in their own concerns, regardless of a blog-site's political orientation. For example, users advertise their own interests and in some cases give links to their own websites, while blogsite developers use them to market their own products. The blogs are clear examples of Chinese netizens behaving as self-focused, self-managing consumers. These practices are quite common, as well-known theoretizations on liberalism and governmentality suggest. The final section of this chapter critiques them with reference to China.

The blogosphere as a means of producing "self-managing consumers"

The practice of blogging in China and the way that censorship operates in the Chinese blogosphere display strong signals of self-regulating behaviour. Self-regulation, in fact, is the ultimate goal of governmentality (see Dean's 2002 genealogy of liberalism, for example). Four types of technology — of production, sign systems, power, and the self — Foucault argues

> permit individuals to effect by their own means or with the help of others a certain number of operations on their own bodies and souls, thoughts, conduct and way of being, so as to transform themselves in order to attain a certain state of happiness, purity, wisdom, perfection, or immortality. (1988a, p. 18)

In the case of the Chinese blogosphere, what we see is the empowerment of free yet governable subjects (Rose 1999a, p. 135), who are enabled and sanctioned to navigate the offerings of each BSP to satisfy their own personal desires and consumer wants.

By such means, China has demonstrated hybrid governance in the last three decades, combining Maoist socialism, nationalism and development with "market socialism" within the parameters of the Communist Party (Nonini 2008, p. 146). For example, to manage Chinese bloggers, most of whom are Generation Y Internet users and so different from China's previous generations, the Chinese government is employing different strategies (or "technologies"). Due to Generation Y's distinctive characteristics, such as being self-centred and rebellious, the government employs implicit technologies. Being indirect, these technologies are strategies to shape people's economic or social conduct, individually or via agencies, without shattering people's sense of independence (Miller & Rose 1990, p. 88). The government's overriding task, therefore, is "to do things in the centre that sometimes makes it possible to dominate spatially as well as chronologically the periphery" (Latour 1987, p. 232).

Rose (1999a) believes management of the soul requires the construction of freedom, which seems somewhat paradoxical, but what he means is that self-regulation (freedom) demands self-discipline. This can be fostered through nationally-fostered ideals of what to aim for and become (p. 11).

Foucault (1991) addresses this need for discipline in his theorization of governmentality, in which he draws on sixteenth-century Protestant and Catholic pastoral doctrines of the government of souls and lives, as well as the general government of the state by Machiavelli's Prince, to foreground obedience and submission to authority through ritualization of personal behaviour (p. 87). In the case of the Chinese blogosphere, while freedom of expression has expanded from apolitical to political topics, in those now "free" spaces, the state retains the right to accredit and provide the necessary symbols of authority and state power. In short, the state encourages nationalism through manipulating online populations; it does this by encouraging consumerism as individual choice (Powell & Cook 2007, p. 139).

In China, then, so-called free spaces for individuals to pursue personal interests as well as purchase merchandise and services are managed by government strategies, which simultaneously encourage and constrain debates on nationalism and patriotism. So promoting a consumerist culture can be used to wake up nationalistic passions about the Dalai Lama and CNN's negative coverage at the same time. To channel people's attention in such ways is a significant means of stabilizing the current party's power. Consequently, the next chapter focuses specifically on how nationalistic discourse has developed in China and how the newest wave of Chinese nationalism differs from previous ones.

PART II

Analyzing Chinese Anger

3

三

Anger as a Display of Nationalism

Promotion of consumerism

Recent literature suggests that the Chinese government welcomes the anger that Chinese bloggers have displayed at Western media criticism of censorship in. The government indirectly or otherwise supports consumerism as a legitimate form of freedom for its people in return for loyalty to the state. Chinese Generation Y, in particular, has learned to appreciate the greater social freedom that shopping and communicating on the Internet offers it, compared with that available to earlier generations. This freedom alone has ensured the loyalty of this generation to the Chinese state so far.

The dislike of Western ideology has been a consistent theme in displays of Chinese nationalism and loyalty since 1989 (Gries 2004; Zheng 1999), but the anger Chinese bloggers have demonstrated towards the Western media more recently indicates a new attitude, a willingness to consume products of Western culture yet resentment of Western political ideology. While increasing numbers of Chinese consume Western products such as Starbucks' coffee, wear Adidas shoes, earn Western degrees and, even, become permanent residents of Western countries, love for motherland China is also growing stronger.

Loving one's motherland is not only a Chinese phenomenon. But among the Chinese, love for the motherland is mainly an expression of support for the central government, and it persists despite widely-exposed corruption at local government level. How has this support for the national government come about?

Changing Chinese attitudes to nationalism

Between 1949 and 2008, the history of China reveals four phases of nationalism that are distinguishable by differing attitudes among its people towards the West. These 60 years demonstrate economic progress in China and, particularly recently, satisfying, individual prosperity. Chinese people call the suffering of defeats in a series of military confrontations with the West and Japan in the century preceding this period the "Century of Humiliation".

Starting from the mid-1800s, the following one hundred years gave impetus to the Chinese nationalism that followed (Zhao 2004, p. 50).

Let me as an ethnic Chinese person explain why that earlier time is called the "Century of Humiliation". In 1636, the Manchus renamed their kingdom Qing and took over China from the Han. The rulers of the Qing Dynasty viewed the Emperor as the Son of Heaven and the Chinese considered themselves as the centre of the universe (Tyson 1995, p. 116). The Chinese name for China, Zhongguo, translates as "The Middle Kingdom", illustrating the Chinese feeling of being the centre of the universe. The Qing Dynasty looked upon foreigners as barbarians, and hence did not want to open up China to trade with other countries (Wang 1998). Although in 1757 Qing rulers declared Guangzhou in Canton would be the only legal port for foreign trade, this strict foreign trade policy strained relationships between China and other countries (Dillon 1998, p. 38).

As a consequence, the Qing Dynasty encountered many problems during the nineteenth century when China also lost both Opium Wars. These defeats precipitated China's economic and military decline. Due to heavy war loans and debts, the Qing government had to increase taxes to pay for the war but also had to accept foreign trade (Scott 2007, p. 11). Burgeoning foreign trade led to the opening up of China and simultaneously initiated China's century of humiliation, its "bainian guochi", which lasted until World War Two. During this painful time, China had to sign a series of unequal treaties with Western countries and Japan, which cumulatively weakened both the country's territorial integrity and its sovereignty (Wang 1998).

Before and during these difficult times, the Chinese nation had neither an official name nor a real national flag; nor did it exhibit any of the elements that normally symbolize a nation-state. Liang Qichao, one of the most influential Chinese scholars and journalists of that time, wrote "Nothing makes me more ashamed than the fact that our nation has no name" (1989a, p. 3). Liang (1959, p. 35) and Hsu (1960, p. 69) observed that the Chinese people had no conception of what a nation-state might be until their defeat in the Sino-Japanese War.

China's defeat at the hands of its old enemy Japan occurred at the same time that China was forced to concede Hong Kong and other territories to Britain and various European powers. These events awakened China from its "great dream of four thousand years" (Liang 1989b, p. 113). After this tumultuous period, Chinese people realized not only that China was not the Middle Kingdom of the world but also that other entities in the world considered themselves its equal, identifying themselves as nation-states with national sovereignty (Wei & Liu 2001, p. 102–3).

The period of the Sino-Japanese conflict thus demonstrated the importance of constructing a strong national identity through a powerful nation-state, a model that could underpin China's developing nationalism in the future. Unlike in Europe, where nationalism had been internally "driven by the combined force of mercantilism and liberalism, nationalist consciousness in China was triggered by external stimulus" (Zhao 2004, p. 50). As a result, the term "Zhonghua minzu" (Chinese people or nation) tends to be tightly linked to nationalistic fears of national annihilation under external invasion (Dittmer & Kim 1993, p. 252).

Overall, such events combined to ensure that Chinese nationalism would contain strong anti-foreign sentiment. But how should the rise of Chinese Generation Y's resentment to the West be understood today? Is it a continuation of the old anti-foreign sentiment or does it represent something new? Considering these questions is central to an understanding of modern Chinese nationalism, which began when the Chinese Communist Party (the CCP) took power in 1949 and founded the People's Republic of China.

Analyzing Chinese nationalism between 1949 and 2008 is more complex, however, because nationalism is an ambiguous term. For the purposes of this particular study, I divide Chinese nationalism from 1949 to 2008 into four phases: the Mao era (1949–1976); after Mao's death and before the Tiananmen Square incident (1976–1989); from the Tiananmen Square incident until China was elected to host the 2008 Olympics (1989–2001); and the period of preparation for and hosting the Beijing Olympics (2001–2008). I focus on Chinese attitudes towards Western ideologies in each period and the exercise of governmental power in forming these attitudes.

In 1949, the CCP founded the new China on the basis of anti-Japanese sentiments. The CCP has built its legitimacy on its nationalistic credentials ever since. Hence, Chinese nationalism is expressed as a "victor narrative" of heroic Chinese victories over Western and Japanese imperialism at that time (Gries 2005, pp. 105–6). The nationalistic sentiments continued the CCP's anti-imperialist drive but more importantly reflected, from the top down, strong worship for the leader Chairman Mao Tse-tung due to Mao's mythic/heroic-image-building strategy (Chang 2003). Mao is widely credited with restoring China's dignity:

> Mao stood atop the Gate of Heavenly Peace in 1949 and proclaimed that "The Chinese people have stood up", thus visually illustrating his point while further fusing his image with the national identity of the Chinese people. (Kluver 1996, p. 28)

The CCP, then, came to power on the basis of anti-Western and anti-Japanese imperialism in 1949. The Party subsequently portrayed the USSR as the model for "the dreamland" which would follow the building of the new Chinese nation (Wei, Liu & Kirby 2002, p. 83). The CCP followed its Soviet Union brother's revolutionary journey by adopting the Marxist-Leninist doctrine of nationalism, namely, that political behaviour can be reduced to economic interests (Zheng 1999, p. 69). According to this doctrine, nationalism is either a disguised economic interest or, in Marxist terms, false consciousness that misleads people and stops them from pursuing their real class interests.

The whole country was enthusiastic for close connections with the Soviet Union: invitations to Soviet specialists became national policy, and every area of administration was open and ready for Soviet instruction (Wei, Liu & Kirby 2002, pp. 83–6). But Mao soon found such apprenticeship to conflict seriously with the Chinese nationalistic goal — that is, to build a strong and independent nation-state — and so China's honeymoon with the Soviet Union ended in 1960. The CCP consequently substituted patriotism for nationalism and articulated the goal to create a strong national state that all Chinese could identify with (Zheng 1999, pp. 69–70). Mao's ideology of patriotism can be interpreted as anti-imperial, anti-feudal, anti-Confucian and anti-capitalist (Zhang 2001, p. 264). Combined with his mythic image, Maoist ideology helped to stabilize the CCP government and legitimize its new policies.

Scholars have described Mao as the greatest hero of the Chinese national epic (Chang & Halliday 2005; Kluver 1996; Teiwes 1996). The Cultural Revolution, which brought chaos to the nation, illustrates the rhetorical power of Mao's mythic image best. Jung Chang describes the mysterious cult of Mao in her memoirs of growing up during the Cultural Revolution:

> Mao made himself more godlike by shrouding himself in mystery. He always appeared remote, beyond human approach … Mao, the emperor, fitted one of the patterns of Chinese history: the leader of a nationwide peasant uprising who swept away a rotten dynasty and became a wise new emperor exercising absolute authority. And, in a sense, Mao could be said to have earned his god-emperor status. He was responsible for ending the civil war and bringing peace and stability … It was under Mao that China became a power to be reckoned with in the world, and many Chinese stopped feeling ashamed and humiliated at being Chinese. (Chang 2003, p. 137)

After the death of Mao in 1976, Deng Xiaoping introduced a modernization program to make China stronger and richer, and between 1976 and 1989 Chinese nationalistic sentiment could be described as pro-Western. During this phase and before the crackdown in 1989 on the mass public protests in Tiananmen Square, coordinated efforts to support individuals and their living requirements — referred to as "pastoral power" (Dean 1991, p. 81) — were implemented. This reform and the policy of opening China to the West in the 1980s meant that the living standards of Chinese people improved significantly due to the rapid economic growth that ensued. Between 1981 and 1991, for example, the percentage of household colour television sets increased from less than one per cent to 70 per cent of the population (Zheng 1999, p. 50). Meanwhile, Western ideas, including that of democracy, flourished in China.

Traditionally, the defining features of democracy comprise all citizens having equal access to power, exercising equal control over state matters through consensus, and enjoying formal equality of rights and privileges under a system of law. However, democracy is also time- and situation-specific, affected, for example, by how a state organizes government and divides or consolidates power in response to internal and external factors. There have been three major types of democracy in the West (Keane 2009), starting with participatory democracy such as the ancient Greek assemblies. Representative democracy, a more indirect governmental structure, has many variants in the West, for example, the US and the UK. A monitory democracy is the model to which China came closest in the 1980s. This form is characterized by scrutiny of power-based organizations, for example, human rights organizations, integrity commissions, and citizens' assemblies. In other words, monitory democracy regulates and reinforces specific balances of power between citizens and the government. But the Chinese government now appears to believe that shared power could weaken the party and that democracy, therefore, might cause societal chaos.

According to a nationwide survey in 1987 (Min 1989), 75 per cent of Chinese were tolerant of the inflow of Western ideas, and 80 per cent of Chinese Communist Party members held a similar attitude (p. 128). Moreover, due to the fast-growing economy, the desire of

Chinese intellectuals for democracy in China became intense. These scholars believed that the traditional culture of China hindered the country's democratization and that the future of China depended on thorough westernization (Su et al. 1988). The erection of the Chinese nationalists' statue of the Goddess of Democracy during the Beijing Spring in 1989 speaks of their desire to promote democracy in China (Gries 2004, p. 6).

The 1989 democratic movement did not succeed. For Chinese leaders, the purpose of political reform was not to weaken the Party but to stabilize it (Zheng 1999, p. 50). So the 1989 popular movement, which ended in Tiananmen Square, caused a return to the exercises and excesses of sovereign power. Meanwhile, the sustained economic development in the 1990s also began to satisfy Chinese people's individual needs. In these ways during this time, Chinese nationalistic sentiments were shaped both top down and bottom up. After the Tiananmen Incident in 1989, and especially after Jiang Zemin assumed power in 1992, nationalism was promoted as a dominant discourse in China and it was in this era that Chinese nationalists' attitudes became hostile towards the West.

Overall, Chinese government's promotion of nationalism was due to several factors, including the collapse of European communism, Chinese re-evaluation of Western culture, and a society that was changing more quickly than prevailing ideology (Zheng 1999, pp. 51-2). First, what happened in the Soviet Union and Eastern Europe influenced the traditional thinking of Chinese intellectuals, who expressed the following kind of view:

> [S]ocial disintegration is a more serious threat to China than social stagnation and conservatism, that political and social chaos will follow the decline of the traditional ideology and the worsening of social crises. Therefore, it … [is] necessary to promote nationalism as a new ideology. (Sun 1996, p. 17 [translated in Zheng 1999, p. 51])

Second, Chinese intellectuals started criticizing the West and its possible influences on China. Whereas before 1989 they believed China should become westernized, in the 1990s westernization was considered to be having negative effects on Chinese traditional culture. In addition, the Chinese questioned the West's intentions towards the rise of China, particularly since the West wanted to impose stringent conditions on China's entry into the World Trade Organization (WTO) (Sun 1996, p. 17). Third, the old, more expansive ideology of reform and opening-up that began in 1978 had become outdated and less relevant in Chinese thinking. A new ideological tool was needed to manage the changing society, and nationalism was the best candidate (Chen 1996, p. 74).

Interestingly, Chinese nationalists in this phase appeared to favour the victimization narrative of the Century of Humiliation (Gries 2004, p. 4). Accordingly, they questioned the inflow of Western culture that started flooding China in the late 1990s. In 1997, Song Qiang, the author of the nationalistic book *Unhappy China*, reflected on the materialism of his generation: "Cultural and spiritual fast food has taken over" (1997, p. 23). Generation Y seemed to believe it must defend China's stability whereas the generation before 1989, according to Generation Y, was dangerously romantic and radical (Gries 2004, p. 5). The May 8 nationalistic protests and demonstrations of 1999 illustrate this in their use of a painting of a skeleton of the statue of liberty — a sharp contrast to 1989's Goddess of Democracy.

However, it is important to note that although Chinese nationalists demonstrated their resentment of Western liberty in this era, the desire for democracy still existed. What Chinese nationalists resisted were the Western models of democratization and theories of development. They believed Westernization was the cause of China's national and cultural identity crises. China's modernization, they believed, should be separated from Westernization, and the future development of China should rely instead on "Chinesenization" (Zheng 1999, p. 53).

The anti-Westernization narrative strengthened even further after 2001 with the maturity of China's post-80s generation and the inspiring Chinese achievements of 2001: Beijing was elected to host the 2008 Olympics, Shanghai hosted the Asia-Pacific Economic Cooperation (APEC) meeting, China successfully joined the WTO, and China's national football team got a pass to the World Football Cup for the first time in China's history. The China Economy Website called this first year of the twenty-first century the "Chinese year" and saw it as a very good sign for China in the new century (China Economy Website 2009). The issue of China's national and cultural identity crises due to Westernization promoted in the previous wave of nationalism was gradually replaced by a new wave of pride and a victory narrative.

The resurgence of Chinese nationalism manifested by the young Chinese generation after 2001 not only captured major worldwide attention in 2008 but also demonstrated something powerful and different: overwhelming, intense pride in the country and its central government. Concurrently, and even more distinctively, the inflow of Western "cultural and spiritual fast food" questioned by the previous generation of nationalists is beloved by this latest generation. In the minds of Generation Y, the anti-West ideology has shifted from a clear anti- or pro-Western attitude to paradoxical attitudes about the West: extreme embrace of Western culture on the one hand, sharp resentment of Western political ideologies on the other.

The Internet as a tool of expression for this generation's nationalistic sentiments has become a distinguishing feature of the victory wave because this generation is the first to grow up with the Internet in China. While consumerist behaviour dominates the Internet, largely through the young generation's online activities (see Chapter Two), the Internet also spreads and strengthens the passion for issues that involve China's political image.

The 2008 anti-CNN campaign (introduced in Chapter 1 and the focus of Chapter 6) illustrates the latest Chinese nationalistic sentiment. The anti-CNN forum expressed high emotions after CNN's coverage of Tibet and other Western coverage of the Olympic torch relay in 2008. These events enabled young Chinese people via MSN messenger to express both their love for China and their support for the Beijing Olympic Games. Netizens added the symbol of a red heart against their MSN names and placed the English word "China" next to itXiao, Wu& Chen 2008. The consistent, continuous act of expressing "love China" via MSN demonstrated united Chinese opposition to the Western media's coverage of the Beijing Olympic Games protests. Generation Y's actions on the Internet represented a new Chinese national identity, composed of resentment of the West and intense pride of China, and its actions are quite distinctive from earlier waves of Chinese nationalism.

Strategic use of government power

Studying the Chinese government's management strategies facilitates understanding of how the Chinese people view China as a nation. Foucauldian analysis, for example, indicates that nationalism and political power are generally so closely aligned so as to form inseparable ties. For example, political movements seeking to exercise state power often validate their actions with nationalistic arguments (Breuilly 1993, p. 1). Nationalism by some is held to be a political movement by definition (e.g. Brass 1991) and so capable of transforming political situations (Hobsbawm 1983). Anderson (1991) proposed close analytical links between nationalism and ethnicity through two profoundly contrasting chains of connections called "serialities" (p. 11), which could be bound or unbound. However, government roles are critical in any analysis of modern nationalism and "bound" governmental chains are capable of creating a sense of community — and hence the development and politics of ethnic identity. Anderson argues further, however, in his study of Indonesia in *Imagined Communities*, that nationalism can generally be aligned with the "large cultural systems that precede it" — in Indonesia's case, "the religious community and the dynastic realm" (Anderson 1991, p. 12). Although the case of Indonesia is somewhat different from that of China in many respects, Anderson's methodology of analyzing print media, maps, census surveys, and museums illustrates how an analytic focus on techniques of government can help to develop understanding of the forces and influences that underpin nationalism.

Foucault's governmentality approach encompasses a similar theme to that of Anderson. Foucault argues that any analysis of nationalism falls inevitably within the framework of governmentality. In his analysis of power relations and the processes of government, he describes societies as demonic because they operate through two games that have the potential for conflict, the citizen game and the shepherd-flock game (1988b, p. 71). The interplay of these two games frequently forms the story of the modern state.

The identification of pastoral and sovereign power in Foucault's approach also mirrors Anderson's analysis of large cultural systems. Eudaily (2004) suggests that configurations such as these provide unique analytic tools (p. 40).

Given the importance of Foucault's analysis and the related approaches outlined above, it is worth contemplating what he means by pastoral and sovereign powers. According to Foucault, sovereign power, which denotes legal enforcement of citizen responsibilities (see Dean 1991), tends to be centralized and repressive, its laws derived from the rule of kings. A diagram of sovereign power, therefore, places the sovereign head outside the political system (Eudaily 2004, p. 39). By comparison, pastoral power links individual needs and state obligations to society and people's personal, moral salvation (Dean 1991, pp. 81–2). Thus, unlike centralized sovereign power that colonizes top-down, pastoral power is exercised through more personalized strategies intended to have individual effects "by attributing, in an essential paradox, as much value to a single lamb as to an entire flock" (Foucault 1983, p. 219). Diagrams of pastoral power thus locate a moral, reflective ethos at a state's centre. Tactical exercise of power by institutions, is what Foucault calls the "art of governmentality" (Foucault, 1991, p. 3).

So, according to many analysts, there is a close relationship between the concepts of nationalism and governmentality according to many analysts. For the purposes of this study, using the concepts Foucault refers to as pastoral power and sovereign power makes it possible to see a significant change in the exercising of governmental power in China, a change that is enabling Chinese Generation Y to create its own form of nationalism. In Foucauldian terms, the Chinese government has shifted from exercising sovereign power to employing pastoral power.

A new nationalistic perspective

The new wave of nationalistic sentiment, as already argued, demonstrates a startling contrast between earlier, tentative desires for progress towards an open, democratic society in China and current views represented by Generation Y. This generation shows little interest in more political power. Besides, the historical overview (see above) reveals that an interesting relationship between democracy and nationalism operates in China.

After Deng started the post-1976 modernization program, Chinese nationalism became pro-Western. Rapid economic development led intellectuals to call for China to become a democracy. After the failure of the 1989 democratic movement, Chinese nationalists immediately started questioning the inflow of Western culture into China. These thinkers considered themselves realistic, pragmatic defenders of stability and order. Although this generation of nationalists did not bring China democracy either, the desire for democracy still existed. However, the new wave of Chinese nationalism represented by China's Generation Y born after 1980 has marked a real change.

The relationship between Chinese nationalism and democracy is not a new topic. The interrelationship of nationalism, the state, and Chinese democratization is complex and since the 1990s scholars have pointed out that nationalistic sentiment in China tends to conflict with any push for democracy in disputes over national boundaries (Chang 1998; He & Guo 2000; Sautman 1997). While post-Mao, analysts mostly assumed Chinese citizens' desire for democracy and admitted the democratic potential of nationalism in China (He 2003; Wang 2003), the latest wave of Chinese nationalism displayed by Generation Y appears to contradict these previously positive attitudes.

In short, resistance to structural change characterizes the latest wave of Chinese nationalism. As Chapter 2 analyzed, the post-1980 generation in China is the first generation to grow up in a consumerist society and have the Internet, and many young people are spoiled at home because they are the only child. The current levels of reform and opening up have satisfied many of their curiosities about the world. Their everyday lives contain Western elements — Coca-Cola, Hollywood movies, iPods — and they appear to have little interest in participating in political changes. They form a generation for whom, since prosperity and personal freedom are achievable, democracy is not required. One member of Generation Y explains the response as follows:

> our life is pretty good. I care about my rights when it comes to the quality of a waitress in a restaurant or a product I buy. When it comes to democracy and all that, well … [t] hat doesn't play a role in my life. (Elegant 2007)

But to what extent is Generation Y's nationalistic sentiment and resentment towards the West free of the government's intervention or influence? As the earlier analysis has already intimated, to assume that it is free of it would be to oversimplify the reality. Accordingly, I propose that China's Generation Y's nationalistic sentiments are stimulated through the government's promotion of the online consumer culture. In the next section, I articulate this argument, starting by considering prevailing Western and Chinese interpretations of Chinese nationalism.

The interpretation of Chinese nationalism

The problem of understanding Chinese nationalism is inflamed by continuing debate on the role that the Chinese government plays in shaping nationalism (Zhao 2004, pp. 12–14). Some scholars argue that Chinese nationalism is driven from the bottom up and that the emergence of Chinese nationalism is the will of the people for the development of the nation. Others believe that it is imposed from the top down by the state as an expression of the interests of the CCP.

The dominant Western perception: "Top down"

The dominant Western view defines Chinese nationalism as an expression of the interests of the ruling elite, that is, the interest of the communist state in Chinese nationalism. One view is that nationalism is a means of defending the state from foreign influences:

> The Chinese do not have an inspired version of nationalism based on shared ideals and worthy principles.... They are left with only a keen sense of "we-ness versus they-ness", an outlook that can only serve xenophobic passions. (Pye 1996, p. 67)

Enforcement of nationalism is the legal prerogative of the state, which the CCP exercises, for example, by manipulating national symbols. In this way, the central government can be said to play "a determining role in the construction and management of a national identity dynamic." (Dittmer & Kim 1993, p. 87)

Meanwhile, perceptions of Chinese nationalism outside the country are based on other understandings of international relations (Zheng 1999, pp. 4–5). In particular, in the West two distinct theories of international relations, realism and liberalism, have had a profound impact on how the international implications of Chinese nationalism are perceived. From the realist perspective, China's nationalism originated in the ending of the Cold War, which allowed new ethnic struggles to surface in the suddenly-created "power vacuum" in East Asia (Buzan & Segal 1994, p. 15). Based on its rapid economic growth and modern development, China was in a position to fill this void (Zheng 1999, p. 5) and its new nationalistic surge provoked palpable anxiety at the possibility of further wars in its neighbours (Kristof 1993; Roy 1995, pp. 48–50).

Liberals believe that war is unlikely among democratic states, but an nregime experiencing such rapid economic development as China is clearly threatening to its neighbours (Doyle 1983; Owen 1994; Russett 1993). Liberals also argue that there is a fundamental difference between how peace is experienced in Europe and in Asia. Most European states are stable democracies with relatively low social and economic differentiation; in Asia such experience is rare. Moreover, regimes in the Asiatic region vary considerably: totalitarian North Korea, South-East Asian countries' combinations of modernizing and authoritarian governments, the liberal democracies of Australia and New Zealand, and China's capitalism with its own characteristics (Friedberg 1993/4, p. 5–33). Liberals further believe that China's advancing nuclear capability poses a great threat to world peace (Buzan & Segal 1994; Segal 1995; Roy 1995).

Although realists and liberals propose different strategies to cope with China's rise to world power they are in agreement on the role that the CCP has played in the growth of Chinese nationalism. The dominant Western interpretation of Chinese nationalism is that "the Communist Party has constructed Chinese nationalism as a tool to legitimize its rule" (Gries 2004, p. 18). In response, realists argue that China's nationalism must be constrained and Chinese power must be balanced. Accordingly, they believe it is in the interest of the United States and other Asian Pacific powers to seek to weaken China by restraining its economic development (Segal 1995, p. 73). On the other hand, liberals believe that China will eventually become democratic so long as its economic and cultural development continues:

> Based on the experience of political development in other East Asian nations, promoting economic growth while monopolizing political power is an almost impossible balancing act over the long term, especially in a world increasingly linked by communications and trade, as people's income rises and their horizon broadens, they are more likely to demand the right to participate in government and to enjoy full protection under the rule of law. (Talbot 1996, p. 57)

But underpinning these differences of views, both liberals and realists believe that the CCP has incited nationalism to maintain its rule in political crises. It has even been argued that "the Chinese Communist Party is no longer communist ... [so] it must be even more Chinese" (Christensen 1996, p. 38). In other words, now that the ideological grip of communism is less strong, nationalism is even more important as a government tool than previously. There is, then, broad consensus in the West that Chinese nationalism today is an important tool frequently utilized by the Communist rulers to stabilize its power: it is "party propaganda" (Gries 2004, p. 18). Thus, the general Western perception of recent Chinese bloggers' hostility to the proliferation of news that is patently not pro-China is that such antagonism is the result of Communist brain-washing. This perception is not entirely inaccurate but in my view it is an oversimplification. Chinese nationalism is more complex than that.

The dominant Chinese perception: "Bottom up"

According to the "bottom up" view, Chinese nationalism is eternal and objective; it reflects the people's attitudes rather than the government's interests (Gries 2004; Zheng 1999). Three clear reasons why Chinese nationalism reflects popular rather than government interest have been proposed:

First, it is about how the Chinese state should and can be reconstructed in accordance with the changing domestic and international circumstances. Second, it is about state sovereignty and people's perception of China's proper position of power in a world of nation-states. Third, it is about people's perceptions of a "just world order", an international system that accords with China's national interest. (Zheng 1999, p. 14)

In other words, Chinese nationalism is not simply party propaganda because Chinese citizens now play a central role in how nationalism is conceived and develops. The Chinese, like all peoples, "have deep-seated emotional attachments to their national identity" (Gries 2004, p. 18, one of very few Western scholars to comment on the link between emotion and nationalism).

Overseas Chinese scholars also argue that the role of the CCP is less influential than is commonly thought (Fong 2004; Zhao 2002; Zhou 2005b). The basis for their argument is that although most overseas Chinese have access to different information and therefore are free from Chinese state intervention, there is no evidence that liberalism, for example, is more popular than nationalism among them. In 2003 and 2004, the anthropologist Vanessa Fong conducted research among young Chinese adults studying in Australia, Ireland, the U.K. and the U.S. Her findings indicate that despite daily exposure to everyday life in the West and Western media perspectives, students expressed a nationalistic Chinese attitude when interviewed about the 1999 bombing of the Chinese embassy in Belgrade (Fong 2004). Her findings echo those of mainland Chinese research, for example, that of sociologist Zhao Dingxin. After interviewing over 1,200 elite university students in Beijing, he claimed that exposure to Western media sources was having little effect on young people's degrees of anger regarding the embassy bombing (Zhao 2002).

I am myself one of China's Generation Y, and living overseas with the opportunity to closely observe the young generation's lifestyle at home and abroad, I agree that liberalism does not appear to be more popular than nationalism among young Chinese. Since the reasons for this are not clearly understood, they are worth deeper consideration.

I argue in this book that to date this phenomenon has been neglected in studies of nationalism among China's Generation Y, and further, that an explanation may be found through studying the Chinese state's tactics of governmentality, that is, why the government chooses to encourage some forms of self-sufficiency and independence ("technologies of the self" in Foucault's terms) rather than employ the machinery of propaganda.

Bridging the difference: The CCP's governmentality tactics

It is possible to claim that the consequences of the Cultural Revolution and the Tiananmen Square incident caused Chinese Generation Y's current apathy to democracy, so that there was no need for the CCP to seek to influence young people's attitudes to it. When Generation Y's parents talk about the chaos of the Cultural Revolution, the horror stories their children hear may alone be sufficient to make them apolitical. Most parents warn their children never to join alternative political movements in China. In any case, regardless of such advice, the chapter of political unrest and confrontation in Chinese history is ancient history to most of the young generation. What Generation Y has witnessed and experienced with its own eyes are a peaceful China and the country's economic boom. Some members of Generation Y have vague memories of the Tiananmen Square protest in 1989, but they tend to believe that such protests are no longer needed and would actually be counter-productive:

> If popular uprisings like Tiananmen were allowed to continue, they would have provoked a counteraction by conservative forces and led to a return to fortress China: no more iPods, overseas shopping trips or snowboarding weekends. (Elegant 2007)

The preference for iPods and shopping over democracy also raises something else worthy of consideration: Among this Internet-savvy, pragmatic younger generation, how could nationalistic sentiment be formed by external factors if it is not also their natural emotion? And if it was formed by external factors, for what purposes?

It is certainly not simply party propaganda from the top anymore, because the CCP does not openly talk about nationalism. In fact, the Chinese government is cautious about evoking nationalistic sentiment because it is aware that Chinese nationalism is a double-edged sword that could one day turn against the government itself, as it did in demonstrations against the American government embassy in 1999, and the Japanese government embassy in 2004 when violent protests by aggressive Chinese anti-Japanese demonstrators erupted on the streets of Shanghai and dozens of other Chinese cities for several days (Zhao 2005).

Hence, the Chinese government knows that nationalism poses a potential threat to the current political framework. This may explain why in the case of anti-CNN protests in 2008 there were no street demonstrations in domestic China at all. The anti-CNN case, a clinching episode for the argument of this book, is analyzed in Chapter 6.

But to explain nationalism as arising solely out of an emotion from below that comes from the Chinese people themselves is also too simple. The CCP does have a nationalist strategy, but it is more sophisticated than previously acknowledged. The CCP has awoken nationalistic sentiments through promoting a consumerist culture, and it is this strategy that has enabled it to penetrate to the roots of Chinese consciousness. By encouraging the pursuit of personal economic freedom as an ultimate goal, nationalism is stimulated at the same time. This effect is particularly evident in Chinese cyberspace, where much consumerist activity and social interaction now occurs. In this sphere, political strategies can be waged more subtly than in any direct state or policing interventions. Thus, nationalism can be engendered by the state through a complex range of strategies, an array of "technologies" connecting the strategic calculations of the political centre and a state's institutions to thousands of micro-locales where individual or group conduct is shaped (Rose 1999b, pp. xxi–xxii). But why does the Chinese government need to do this?

Why encourage nationalistic sentiments in China today?

There are two main reasons why China has sought to stimulate national sentiment via the promotion of consumerism during the recent period of China's phenomenal economic growth. One explanation is, as already mentioned (Section 3.4 above), the mismatch between old ideologies and the needs of a fast-changing society. Renewed appeals to nationalistic sentiment were required to stabilize the government and legitimize the government's policies for China's future. Linking the Party directly to the nation meant that in people's consciousness, "love of country" automatically became "love of Party" (Link 2008, p. 6). There were particular advantages to the current party in following this strategy. Take, for example, the two bids to host the Olympics:

> If a bid were successful (as it was in 2001), the glory would rebound to the Party; if unsuccessful (as in 1993), foreigners could be blamed for disrespecting the Chinese nation—and this, too, would pull the Party closer to the people. (Link 2008, p. 7)

Secondly, to promote consumerist culture by nationalizing it is to draw attention away from existing domestic complaints. The growing wealth that online consumerism reflects has also drawn attention to the gaps between rich and poor to the extent that they form a sub-theme in Chinese cyberspace against privilege. The emergence of this sub-theme demonstrated the need to nationalize consumer culture, to unite people rather than divide them. "Getting rich first" is a motto for most Chinese, because money and the power it can bring are two life goals which currently bring special privilege to some people in China. Therefore, those who are not so privileged tend to resent those who are while also desiring to attain those same privileges they resent in others. Thus, envy and resentment mix together to create the "anti-privilege" sentiments displayed in Chinese cyberspace. Because the Internet can unite people regardless of distant physical locations, these "anti-privilege" sentiments have quickly magnified in recent years, forming a virtual but substantive sub-discourse community in Chinese cyberspace, one which today has created a binary distinction between "us" and "them" and which is both "intense and passionate" in its recognition of political friends and enemies in China (Dutton 2008, p. 106). In a number of social activism incidents, such as the "human flesh search engine", which is the phenomenon of hunting for wrongdoers by means of blogs and bloggers' offline social connections, innocent people, who are neither rich nor powerful, have been mistakenly targeted as "them".

Because of such socially-divisive domestic problems, at the same time as the government promotes a consumerist ideology it also seeks to weaken the tension between "us" and "them" through encouraging nationalism. For example, in the case of the Dalai Lama, by drawing attention instead to CNN's negative coverage of China, the government is able to focus people's attention on national goals and so stabilize it's power. It is interesting to consider, therefore, how the Party actually does this.

How are nationalistic sentiments formed?

The cases I have mentioned clearly illustrate that young Chinese people have strong national feelings as well as individualist and consumerist tendencies. Nationalistic sentiment and independence may actually be the result of China's emphasis on patriotic education since the early 1990s (Hoffman 2006; Link 2008). For example, autonomy can be encouraged through enabling people to strive for professional qualifications which enable them to serve their country (Hoffman 2006, p. 550).

Certainly, patriotic education is one of the strategies Chinese governmenthas employed, but it cannot be the full explanation of a generation which grew up with the drive for individualism and consumerism yet is rebellious about the educational narrative: members of Chinese Generation Y are far more interested in planning holiday trips than serving their country. Although Hoffman (2006) refers to interviews conducted with some young Chinese who express their desire to serve the country, I take a more sober view of the credibility of this type of interview. First of all, it is disingenuous to trust their statements while also admitting that self-censorship exists in China. Trusting these respondents' statements assumes that they did not self-censor. Secondly, from my own point of view as a young Chinese, when interviewed by a Westerner and knowing the contents of the interview will be publicized, I would always find it wise to be "patriotic".

For such reasons, I would suggest that the young generation's nationalistic sentiments are ultimately formed through "the channel of consumer culture" (Gerth 2003, p. 13). However, nationalism means different things to different people. For some it is the call for "consuming products made in China", in other words, "Chinese people ought to consume Chinese products", a popular slogan in the previous generation which simultaneously imposed serious constraints on the individual (Gerth 2003, p. 15). Now, though, nationalistic consumerism appears rather different when one looks at Chinese bloggers' "shopping report blogs". As I know personally from my Chinese friends, while they add the love-heart to their MSN names, they also buy Western cosmetic products. Nationalization through consumerism now, I suggest, is the wrapping up of the nationalistic sentiments in cultural products that the young generation consume, from pop songs to online games. One example is the very well-known pop song among China's post 80s generation. The song is called "Chinese", and was sung by Andy Lau, one of the most successful singers and film actors in China since the 1990s. Strong pride in being Chinese is very obvious in the song; the lyric has key phrases such as "5000 years history", "8000 miles of mountains and rivers", "humiliation in the past", "stride proudly ahead". Pride of China's ancient history and the pain of the humiliation in this song are clear:

> In the 5000 years of history, many dreams were hiding
>
> Yellow faces, black eyes, we smile eternally
> 8000 miles of mountains and rivers is like a song
> No matter where you are from and where you will go to
> Same tears, same pain, we leave the humiliation in our hearts
> Same blood, same race, we have dreams in the future, let's fulfill them together
> Hand in hand, no difference between you and me, let's stride proudly ahead
>
> Let the world know that we are Chinese.

This pop song is one of the many entertainment pieces that contain strong nationalistic sentiments. While it is popular as an entertainment piece, it also nationalizes the pop culture that the young generation consumes.

Governing at a distance

In this chapter I investigated the new characteristic of Chinese bloggers' nationalistic sentiments: their embrace of Western culture alongside their resentment of Western political ideology. The chapter made transparent how different the new anti-West national sentiment is in comparison with its predecessors, and how it was formed.

First of all, I examined theoretical conceptions of nationalism and their relationship to governmentality, which entailed examining the procedures and processes a government may put in place to control and manage a state. One technology, or means, for this may be the manipulation of nationalistic feelings. In the case of China, nationalism is loaded with specific cultural and historical resonances, particularly following the founding of the PRC in 1949. The analysis in this chapter made links between the central government and the latest wave of Chinese nationalism, demonstrated by China's young generation, which attracted worldwide attention in 2008.

My main aim was to suggest that Generation Y's nationalistic sentiments do not indicate that the structural changes needed for democracy to occur in China are either desired or likely to happen at the present time. China's Generation Y is happy, or at the very least, content with the current political framework in China. My other related aim was to bridge Western and Chinese perspectives on this topic. I argued that in studies of nationalism involving young Chinese living in China and overseas their paradoxical attitudes towards the West have been ignored so far. This is regrettable since their feelings may have been influenced by mechanisms under government control, even if only indirectly. Whatever the explanation, Chinese bloggers' hostility towards Western criticism of government-imposed censorship in China challenges previous studies which argue the democratic potential of recent waves of nationalism in China. In Chapter 4, I deepen the analysis of Chinese Generation Y's anger about Western accusations of government censorship and its implications for the potential of democracy in China.

4

四

Chinese Anger at the Label of Censorship

A difference of understanding

According to Western media, freedom of expression remains suppressed in China. This belief was the trigger for bloggers' recent anger in China towards the West. Western attitudes and the anger of Chinese Generation Y indicate that Western media and Chinese Generation Y place different values on freedom of speech. For its part, Chinese Generation Y appreciates that, compared with previous generations, it is allowed considerable freedom of speech. Moreover, the freedoms currently allowed give all Chinese people more opportunities than previously to pursue personal goals. Interestingly, however, the economic freedom offered on the Internet in China has also created a modern consumerist generation that is self-regulating. That is, without centrally-organized controls, Chinese people moderate what they do and say. Foucault would describe them as operating technologies of the self (1988a). In general, then, many Chinese people seem satisfied with the current situation, which gives them limited consumer-focused freedoms within an otherwise unchanged political framework.

Because vast differences are apparent between Chinese and Western people in their understanding and experience of censorship, I reviewed the literature on censorship. I found little scholarly literature published on censorship in China, whereas censorship studies in the West have surged in the last 25 years.

The common theoretical position in the West sees all forms of censorship as limiting freedom of speech. Liberal democracies in the West, indeed, encourage and advocate freedom of expression. By contrast, in China, where censorship has been and is still much tighter than in the West, the majority of present-day Chinese people tend to be satisfied with the existing more relaxed, though still limited, freedom of expression.

This chapter therefore pays special attention to the argument on Chinese nationalism from this perspective, namely, the contrasting interpretations of censorship as revealed by, on the one hand, Chinese Generation Y's resentment of Western perceptions of censorship mechanisms in China and, on the other, the impact of that resentment on nationalistic sentiments. Owing to contemporary Chinese people being allowed more freedom of speech and action than in the past, they are grateful for these personal liberties and proud to be Chinese. For this reason, further structural changes to allow even greater personal freedom is unlikely because the majority of young people in particular, the upcoming governing generation, do not desire it.

Understanding the Chinese tradition of censorship

Censorship practices from 1949 to the current market-oriented economic reforms period in China demonstrate the increased freedoms of speech that contemporary Chinese enjoy along with their increased economic prosperity. While publications on censorship in the West have proliferated in the last 25 years, scholarly literature on censorship in contemporary China remains scarce. The most obvious reason for this is that information about censorship is itself censored in China. Although the Chinese tradition of censorship is of long-standing, "no published Chinese source acknowledges the existence of censorship after 1949" (Chen 1992, p. 569). So, in this section, taking 1949 as a watershed in Chinese history, I will first review Chinese censorship practices before 1949 and then analyze censorship practices from 1949 to the market-oriented economic reforms period.

From the Song Dynasty to 1949

Although publications on censorship are few in China, scholars from around the world have documented Chinese censorship practices in the late-imperial times. For example, Chan (1983) provides a comprehensive overview of state censorship in the Chinese book market; Brook (1988) analyzes the impact of the Qianlong inquisition on the book trade in the Qing Dynasty; Japanese scholar Okamoto, who researched prohibited books in China, discusses the impact of the Qianlong inquisitions at the provincial level (1996), and; Guy (1987) describes how state censorship was manipulated by both scholar-officials and local elites under Qianlong emperors of the Qing Dynasty.

These scholars show that Chinese people have lived with rigorous censorship mechanisms since the Song Dynasty (960–1279) and, most notoriously, during the Qing Dynasty in China (1644–1911).

In China, printing was invented in the Tang Dynasty (618–907) but it was not until the Song Dynasty, which began 50 years or so later, that publishing flourished due to the invention of movable type in the 1040s (Chan 1983, p. 2). As publishing enterprises expanded, the rulers of the Song dynasty, having witnessed the proliferation of books and literature printed by private concerns, started elaborating laws and regulations controlling their publication and circulation (Yao 1979, p. 268). Thus, censorship mechanisms were defensive, deliberate, and direct. During the Middle Ages in the West, their counterparts, monarchs and church officials in Europe, also promulgated laws and regulations on publishing and printing in order to safeguard their prerogatives and interests; these regulations established the foundation for publication laws in modern Europe and North Ameria (Bowker 1912, pp. 10–20).

There were differences in what Western officialdom sought to do, however. The Western laws sought "in part to censor heresy or sedition, and in part to foster literature by protecting publishers against piracy" (Chan 1983, p. 3). Thus, the Western laws specified different kinds of procedures because they reflected different institutions, concepts, traditions and heritage (ibid.), whereas the Song Dynasty's publishing laws were designed simply for the government's benefit.

The Song publication laws provided the groundwork for regulations in later dynasties. The twin aims to protect the state's exclusive privileges in the compilation and dissemination of certain categories of works and literature and enforce the state's censorship and proscription of literary works for reasons of domestic politics and state security were accepted and continued by the dynasties which followed, such as the Mongols of the Yuan (1260–1368), the Chinese of the Ming (1368–1644), and the Manchus of the Qing Dynasty (1644–1911), the most famous and notorious of the last being the Qianlong Inquisition.

The Qing transferred power from the Han to the ruler Qianlong because if printing could create chains of reproduced texts for the Han people, then it was potentially subversive and to be feared. Therefore, Qianlong not only banned the majority of printed books but also prohibited the use of undesirable words across the country (Guy 1987). During the inquisition, intellectuals were beheaded because of their writings. In many cases, their deaths were only due to the use of a single word the emperor considered offensive, as happened, for example, with the death of Hu Zhongzao, a provincial education commissioner (Guy 1987, p. 32). Hu used *zhuo qing* in a poem. *Qing* was the name of the dynasty, and *zhuo* means dirty or muddy. The Qianlong emperor understood Hu to be taking a political position in the then unrest between a Han official (Hu's mentor) and a Manchu official, and Hu was eventually beheaded.

Sometimes in such incidents, the immediate and extended families of the writer would be killed as well. For example, in a poem written by a Han poet to commemorate his late father, Qianlong believed some words were hostile towards the Manchus. Hence, Qianlong decided to excavate the coffin of the poet's father, multilate his corpse, and kill all his descendants (Schmidt 2003, p. 370).

In 1912, Sun Yat-sen successfully led a national revolution and established a new government in Nanjing after the fall of the Qing Dynasty. For the first time in Chinese history, Chinese people were promised freedom of speech, authorship, and publication (Chan 1983, p. 26). However, before the promise was enacted as law, the warlord Yuan Shi Kai replaced Sun as the provisional president and moved the capital to Beijing. The unborn freedom of speech law was aborted in Yuan's drive to become emperor. To realize his ambition for power, he sought to suppress civil liberties and control public speech (for example, in newspapers). Article 11 of his proclamations forbade the publication of any writing, drawing or picture deemed subversive, provocative or harmful to social morals. Similarly, the publication of state documents was restricted if considered harmful to state security.

In 1928, the Nationalist Party gained control of the key provinces of China and established a one-party dictatorship. The Party elaborated a set of regulations to suppress political opposition for the purpose of strengthening the Nationalist Party's power and legitimizing its rule. Outwardly, the Nationalist government planned to keep the show of those democratic principles that Sun had promised in 1912, but in reality the government was determined to maintain absolute control over public expression. Accordingly, the Central Political Committee of the Nationalist Party elaborated new laws and principles to regulate printing and publishing (Sae 1987, p. 98). The Nationalist government assured the public that a new publication law would empower freedom of the press, but its real, disguised aim was the opposite. After the enactment of the new publication law, not only all publication agencies were required to register but specific authorities were also appointed to filter any subversive ideas in publications (Ebrey 1993, p. 506).

From 1949 to the market-oriented Economic Revolution

In 1949, the Communist party led by Mao Zedong established the People's Republic of China. The Mao government, disguised by nationalism and Mao's mythic image, controlled the country completely, nationalizing private enterprise and imposing regulations on people's daily activities (Chan 1983).

But the censorship mechanisms under Mao were different from those of its Soviet brother-in-arms (Kraus 2004, p. 109). The Mao government could not copy the Stalinist model of tight surveillance, the most obvious reason being that China had too large a population. Instead, Mao used the concept of "socialist reconstruction" to control thought, education and individual expression (Zheng 1999, p. 60). Duing this period, Mao's mythic heroic-image-building strategy played a significant role in ideological control. In the era of Mao the Cultural Revolution, which turned the nation upside down, is the clearest illustration of censorship mechanisms that can be classified as the activity of a totalitarian regime.

This chaotic period ended after the Mao regime in 1978 with the emergence of relatively moderate leadership under Deng Xiaoping. Deng Xiaoping seized the opportunity for change and launched market-oriented economic reforms. In comparison with the Mao era, Chinese citizens in the 1980s had much more freedom of expression, including opportunities to debate and investigate social, cultural, and to some degree even political issues of the day (Latham 2007, p. 39). This period of "great intellectual excitement and optimism", however, didn't last long (p. 40). Following the Tiananmen Square crackdown in 1989, the early years of the 1990s returned to a period of anxiety and caution during which political control was tightened and self-censorship prevailed.

After Deng Xiaoping's famous tour of Southern China in 1992, in which he called for faster and more thorough marketization, the media landscape started to change, gradually at first and then at unprecedented speed (Hong 1998). Although capitalist management practices were employed, they were adopted only for commercial purposes. Since in China media organizations are still considered as ideological apparatuses of the state, "[t]he most distinguishable characteristic of the Chinese media in the 1990s … [was] the tension between rapid commercialization and continued ideological control" (Ma 2000, p. 21). The tension led to the current situation "in which rapidly commercializing media industries confront slow-changing power relations" in the political, social and economic sectors (Donald & Keane 2002, p. 3).

To grasp censorship in this period of China, it is necessary to understand something about Chinese political structures. The Communist political structure in China is divided into five geographical and administrative levels: central, provincial, municipal, county, and township. Thus, centralized media administration is the responsibility of the Party's Propaganda Ministry, whose policies are implemented from the centre down through provincial, municipal, county and local levels (Hong 1998, p. 45).

In effect, news outlets across the country at all levels are required to implement and prioritize central government's policies. In other words, Party elites define what is "news" (Womark 1986), enabling the state to maintain tight control over political news (Ma 2000, p. 22). In practice, national media are more heavily censored than local and provincial news sources and any liberalization in China's media due to market forces has tended to be uneven.

For example, print media are subject to more restrictions than electronic media. In general, the news media are more restricted than cultural media, with periodicals, magazines, and books containing cultural materials enjoying more freedom than publications with political content. Recently, personal and social issues have been openly canvassed on radio and TV; such openness would have been unimaginable previously (Zha 1995, pp. 103–5).

Censorship does not only vary regionally in China; some newspapers express different ideologies on different pages. For example, the communist party newspaper *Shenzhen Special Zone Daily*, based in China's first "Capitalist lab", may have its front pages filled with official news stories and policy speeches yet its other pages may be packed with advertisements and sensational news (Ma 2000). Also, since the late 1990s, censorship varies at different times of the day within the same medium or source. For example, on China Central Television (CCTV), while the main daily news at 7.00 pm functions mainly as a party propaganda tool, the afternoon and late-night news enjoy relatively more freedom (Chen & Chan 1998). These patterns observed in the late 1990s continue to this day, although the current situation is complicated by new, more negotiable boundaries and degrees of autonomy. For instance, in nowaday China political news may exhibit a degree of autonomy alongside nonpolitical news that enjoy a high degree of autonomy. This new trend, particularly noticeable in cyberspace, is analyzed in the next chapter.

Thus, although political control still generally prevails in China, with the state continuing to see the media as subject to its governance, contemporary Chinese citizens enjoy much more freedom than in the past. Up until quite recently, Chinese people lived under authoritarian, and at times totalitarian, regimes. Historical records make clear that the Chinese now have "increasing freedom to choose, to consume, and to be self-regulating" (Donald & Keane 2002, p. 8). Politically, their activities remain restricted in many aspects, but economically there has been a consumer revolution. Even in political spheres, though, gradually-increasing online influence has been noted (Zhou 2006; Zheng 2008; Yang 2009), to the extent that Chinese netizens can be said to have noticeably affected Chinese government policy in some cases. But while it is now inaccurate to label China, as Jayasuriya (2001) suggested, an authoritarian liberalism model of governance, it is too soon to conclude that the recent signs of political liberalism in China will lead it towards political democracy.

The concept of censorship in the West

The changing landscape

Although censorship has remained an unspoken word in China, in the West censorship studies have surged since the mid-1980s. Censorship used to be considered unappealing to study, because it followed predictable, venerable divisions, which separated modernists from traditonalists (Post 1998, p. 1). In the past, censorship was mainly concerned with obscenity and the undermining of national security. However, new scholarship has burgeoned in the West, such that "high-profile publishers are producing books about censorship, even reference works and bibliographies on censorship have come out, and academic journals are running special editions on it" (Muller 2004, p. 2).

What has caused the revival of censorship studies in the West? Based on the work of Burt (1994) and Muller (2004), the following reasons for this growth can be proposed:

1. *The availability of material*: With the implosion of the Soviet Bloc between 1989 and 1991, a large amount of confidential data came into the public domain and available to researchers.

2. *The right-wing agenda of the Reagan/Bush administrations in the US*: Beginning with the election of Reagan in 1980s, the Regan and Bush administrations started trying to restrict liberty (for example, in aesthetic and ethical areas). These moves raised academic interest in censorship studies in the US, leading to new academic publications on censorship issues, such as political correctness, hate speech, ethnic minorities, pornography, feminism, and terrorism.

With the alterations in the landscape of censorship, understanding of the concept itself has also changed dramatically in the West, to the extent that "there seems no longer to be any consensus about what censorship is" (Rosenfeld 2001, p. 117). These fundamental changes in meaning are reviewed next.

Changing meanings

Traditionally, censorship meant "direct forms of political intervention mostly by state and church" (Muller 2004, p. 4). Thus, strictly, it involved repression, mostly centred in court circles (Post 1998, p. 17), which led to the direct removal and replacement of undesired material (Burt 1998, p. 17). Changes to traditional understandings of censorship have taken place on two fronts. First, censorship is no longer viewed as a simple operation (for example, the direct removal of texts) but as a complex operation (for example, involving dispersal). Censorship procedures thus depend on what is being censored. Texts, for example, are not necessarily destroyed but might be changed from one publication form to another, such as from performance to print (Burt, 1998, p. 17), meaning that in a less-than-generally-literate society, for example, fewer people might have access to information or ideas. Such a strategy is technically not removal but replacement, though removal might be the effect for some.

Further, destructive acts, such as book-burning, might be described as symbolic purification rites.

Thus, the second change in describing censorship involved considering how material was censored. Traditionally, censorship was regarded as a state procedure to protect its own power over what went on in the public sphere, usually "a set of concrete measures carried out by someone in a position of authority" (Muller 2004, p. 4). Under this conception, the state directly exercised censorial power over subjects (Post 1998). However, recent research describes censorship as an effect rather than a feature of power: it can form society in unforeseen ways even when it may also deprive subjects of freedoms such as access to public discussion (see Butler 1997).

Historical reasons for these shifts in meaning are not easy to pin down. However, the end of the Cold War undoubtedly has had an effect, notably in the way that scholars used the work of theorists such as Michel Foucault (Post 1998). It is therefore important to consider the influence of Foucault on current interpretations of the meaning and stratagems of censorship.

A Foucauldian framework of analysis

Foucault himself always saw power as a productive force, something which can be possessed by everyone. Censorship, as a feature of power, therefore, can also be productive, for example, shaping constructions of knowledge and social practice positively (compare Butler 1997, p. 252; Post 1998, p. 2).

For example, pastoral power over society can be productive (Caputo 2006, p. 252) because it links individuals into the collective through discursive frameworks and social practices (Dean 1991). Consequently, individuals, instead of feeling forced to obey a sovereign power, see conforming to societal expectations as their personal duty to obey (Dean 1991, pp. 81–2). For example, when a film and literature censorship board determines which materials will be accessible to the public, individuals may view its decisions as morally correct and so reasonable to accept. In this way, censorship has the capacity to form subjects, which is not the same as repression. Censorship, therefore, "produces reality; it produces domains of objects and rituals of truth" (Foucault 1977, p. 194).

Thus, changing understandings of censorship demonstrate what Foucault terms the "art of governmentality", often indirect control, such as this book demonstrates concerning the Chinese government's regulation of nationalistic sentiment. In a Foucauldian framework, government involves the regulation of and for individuals, that is, as Foucault expresses it, the "conduct of conduct" (Gordon 1991, p. 2). Thus, political theoreticians such as Foucault analyze the taken-for-granted and generally unquestioned practices of government and rule in order to make sense of the concept of power.

Moreover, govermentality is a subtle art. Government regulation, direct and indirect, does not necessarily aim to

> control, subdue, discipline, normalize, or reform … [subjects] but also to make them more intelligent, wise, happy, virtuous, healthy, productive, docile, enterprising, fulfilled, self-esteeming, empowered, or whatever. (Rose 1998, p. 12)

Similarly, the exercise of censoring may not just concern removing undesired material but also disseminating desirable material. So the practice of censorship is more complex than a central state mechanism for governing; it may also include political, military, economic, educational, theological, medical and other sectors of governance and influence (Besley 2006, p. 21). When governments employ a range of tactics and techniques to achieve their goals, their behaviours of governing, their governmentalities, are more or less subtle, making them more or less artful (Dean 1999, p. 18).

Political interpretations of censorship

Other analysts have tended to use simple dichotomies to distinguish censorship — namely, defensive and offensive; structural and deliberate; direct and subtle, and; censorship and self-censorship — but binary distinctions do not reflect the subtle complexities of most political contexts. In the case of China, for example, censorship mechanisms can be described as structural, indirect, defensive and offensive at the same time, as well as encouraging self-censorship. These descriptions may differ at each level of government as well. For example, a censorship mechanism may be introduced by the central government, but by the time it reaches local levels of administration, in some regions it may still be direct and offensive while

Censorship	Technologies			Example
	Power	Self	CP*	
Defensive	✓			The filtering system in Chinese cyberspace bans the posting of some sensitive words
Offensive	✓			The pro-China campaign in 1996 in America
Structural	✓	✓	✓	In an election campaign, a commercial TV station decides to disseminate Candidate A's views instead of Candidate B's because Candidate A can purchase expensive advertisements
Deliberate	✓			An editor bans an article because it offends the government's censorship laws
Direct	✓			Internet laws around the world that cause the imprisonment of people who breach them
Subtle	✓	✓	✓	A TV station pursuing profit by broadcasting the most market-desired programs, and therefore censoring the less desired or undesired programs
Self-censorship	✓	✓	✓	A person who does not want to talk about sensitive political issues because it is the only way to ensure obtaining a grant from the government

CP = Contact points between technologies of power and self

Table 4.1: Technologies of censorship

elsewhere it is being managed by self-censorship. Moreover, the four binaries are sometimes four ways of saying very similar things.

Considering Foucault's analysis (1993) of technologies of power and the self, I re-categorized the binaries according to the "technologies" they employ (Table 4.1). As the examples of censorship provided below will illustrate, what Foucault calls the "contact point" between "technologies of power" and "technologies of the self" (1988a, p. 19) reflects the subtle complexities of most political contexts.

Censorship by power

Defensive, offensive, deliberate, and direct

In essence, in some political contexts, the exercise of censorship entails technologies of power to decide the conduct of individuals (Foucault 1988a, p. 18). Censorship traditionally interpreted as involving removal and replacement of material, a mechanism that prevents information from reaching the public (Burt 1998, p. 17), can be called defensive censorship (Phillips & Harslof 1997, p. 148) — for example, the filtering system in Chinese cyberspace banning the posting of more than 1,000 words.

Offensive censorship also employs technologies of power; it includes the promotion of desirable information to an elite or the mass. Such promotion may involve flooding "the public with a particular version of reality" (ibid.), for example, the pro-China campaign in 1996. Due to China's reputation for human rights violations, child labour and prison-camp abuses, the public relations firm Hill and Knowlton was hired by some Fortune 500 companies to secure China's trade status as a "most favored nation" among the public (Robert 1997). A more recent offensive was the government's handling of SARS in China in 2003.

Even though SARS was spreading throughout China, China Daily's website published a Chinese Foreign Ministry announcement stating the virus was under control and patients in Guangdong province were recovering. Patently, this did not turn out to be the case.

Direct censorship is similar to deliberate censorship or what Bourdieu (1991) calls manifest censorship, which is "imposed by orthodox discourse, the offical way of speaking and thinking about the world" (p. 138). It is explicit, deliberate, radical, and normally punitive: for example, international Internet laws that lead to the imprisonment of people who breach them. In these cases, censorship is a topdown operation carried out by governments and their agents exercising sovereign power.

Censorship by enabling the self

Offensive, structural, subtle, and self-censorship

Structural censorship was first noted by Bourdieu in his essay "Censorship and the imposition of form" (1991). In effect, he defined the exercise of censorship as a commodity market, in which different kinds of expression have different values or prices. According to one's authority in the society, more or less propriety or reticence may be expected. A person's political position acts as a self-regulating force, an example of what Butler (1997, pp. 137–8) calls "implicit censorship", and complements the development of societal norms. Implicit censorship can be good or bad.

For example, during an election campaign, a commercial television station may decide to disseminate Candidate A's views instead of Candidate B's because Candidate A can purchase expensive advertisements, not because Candidate B's opinions need to be censored. Censorship of candidate B is a by-product of his or her financial disadvantage (Cohen 2001, p. 14). At other times, the censorship criteria can be explicit as well as structural: for example, an editor bans an article because it offends against the government's censorship laws.

Subtle censorship also enables the self. For example, in a market economy, what we see and read is not decided by explicit laws, but by market preferences. Commercial publishers and filmmakers, for instance, pursue profit by producing market-desired products, thereby implicitly censoring less desirable items. So in democracies individuals can be "treated as market-led consumers, not as active citizens with rights and obligations." (Keane 1991, p. 91). Importantly, subtle, implicit censorship largely involves technology of the self, another representation of censorship.

Self-censorship is often indirect: for example, a person decides not to say something due to pressure from a third party. The third party could be the government, but it may also be a private interest, or a combination of public and private motivation. For example, Google's censorship in China was due to pressure from the Chinese government, but the consequences of it created the secondary potential of losing a profitable market. Therefore, self-censorship can be intentional and/or unintentional (Cohen 2001, p. 14). A person who decides not to talk about sensitive political issues as the only way of ensuring that he or she obtains a government grant is acting intentionally, whereas a person who maintains silence due neither to private interest nor to government pressure may have unintentionally absorbed societal apathy to political affairs. Self-censorship is more often a conscious choice, however, because normally it affects individuals' interests (Muller 2004, p. 192). When journalists omit small items or drop entire stories they are often acting to secure or advance their own careers.

Naturally enough, there are different interpretations of self-censorship according to political context. The case of Hong Kong, a society in transition, and its understanding of self-censorship is apposite. The Hong Kong Journalists Association and the International Centre Against Censorship based in London jointly formulated a formal definition of self-censorship (Article 19) during Hong Kong's transition from being a British territory to regaining Chinese status:

> The action of individuals or organizations, whether deliberate or routinized and subconscious, in moderating or altering or stifling the expression of their views or the disclosure of information because of a fear — whether real or perceived — of repercussions by China and its various agents and authorities. (HKJA and Article 19, 1997)

The HKJA at the same time identified three broad categories of self-censorship for this transition period:

1. *Direct and indirect external pressures on media organizations*: e.g., channelling advertisement income to China-friendly media is direct commercial pressure;

whereas exerting pressure on media owners with business interests in China, especially on those with a diverse range of business interests, creates indirect pressure on their businesses

2. *Pressure within media organizations*: e.g., the removal of high-risk contributors or contributions such as critical columnists and columns

3. *Individual self-censorship*: e.g., accommodating behaviours by mainland journalists stimulated by fear of arrest.

These self-censorship categories affect the institution, the medium, the organization and the individual (Limor & Nossek 2000). In a specific case in Israel (see Limor and Capsi 1999), the institution exhibiting direct external pressure was the Israeli Press Council, the highest established media authority in Israel. The medium was created by pressure from the Us motion picture industry and the complaints committee of the British press. The organizations were the editorial boards of newspapers, broadcast stations as well as publishers. Individuals were exemplified by any journalist, author, radio or television broadcaster that responded to external pressure intentionally or unintentionally.

Thus, there are many facets to the concept and nature of censorship, which is closely related directly and indirectly to the notion of power and its equally diverse representations. Contact points between the two sets of technologies can subject individuals (Burchell 1996) to the point of repression or create different opportunities. The contact points, however, indicate the nature of governmentality in each case:

> The contact point, where the individuals are driven by others tied to the way they conduct themselves, is what we can call, I think, government. Governing people, in the broad meaning of the word, … is not a way to force people to do what the governor wants; it is always a versatile equilibrium, with complementarities and conflicts between techniques which assure coercion and processes through which the self is constructed or modified by himself. (Foucault 1993, pp. 203–4)

Censorship in various regimes

As would already be clear, the practice of censorship varies according to its political context, rendering any attempt to create a political typology of censorship systems difficult. Whereas Siebert, Schramm and Patterson (1956) delineated four systems — authoritarianism, liberalism, social responsibility and communism — Saeys, some fifty years later, observes an increasingly complex continuum going from one extreme, liberalism, to another, communism (2007, p. 62). However, the extreme communism model applies only to North Korea and perhaps Cuba nowadays, and the boundaries among Siebert et al.'s remaining three systems have become blurred since the 1980s owing to privatization in public sectors and the development of huge media conglomerates (Neveu 2004, p. 331). Most national media institutional practices and most relations between state and media, in fact, display a mixture of libertarian, responsible, and authoritarian elements (McQuail 1994, p. 133). Therefore, to look for simple binary relationships is not productive, although it is worth considering for the moment whether it is possible to simplify such analysis to a sole question, namely, whether a regime is inherently democratic or non-democratic based on its censorship practices.

Theoretically, it can be asserted that censorship is "virtually synonymous with non-democratic regimes" (Limor & Nossek 2000, p. 65). Accordingly, democratic countries may be defined by the value they place on freedoms of all forms of expression. That would be to say, the existence of any censorship mechanism in a regime inherently means that regime would be classified as undemocratic. However, at the same time, one cannot deny that censorship does exist in so-called democratic countries.

The acceptable degree of censorship in democratic states, according to Limor and Nossek (2000), is that which is self-censorship and apparently free from government control. Self-censorship is envisaged as a technology of the self that contributes to balance and stability in society and its democratic values. In the seemingly most transparent democratic regimes, therefore, governments seek to foster self-regulation as their dominant technology of governance; this may include, as already argued above, the regulation of publishable material. This regulation is likely to occur *after* publication in democracies, however, and may also entail guaranteeing reasonable access to information and the media alongside protection for authors (for example, right of reply), and so forth.

Questions of censorship in democratic countries are actually quite complex, although Jansen (1991) has described censorship practices in democracies as being of two main kinds, regulative and constituent. Regulative censorship is deliberately official, prohibitive and punitive; a historical example is the Roman Catholic Church's *Index Librorum Prohibitoreum*, which prohibited the reading of listed texts from 1564 to 1967 (p. 133). Constituent censorship is a more subtle, self-conscious exercise employing different levels of self-consciousness (see above) according to individuals' understandings of and stances on community norms. Hence Foucault's emphasis on the contact points between technologies of power and the self, which lead to continual strategic calculations in all the millions of micro-locales where individual or group conduct is shaped (Rose 1999a, p. xxi-xxii). In reality,

> [i]n a liberal democracy, where censorship is said to be minimal, censorship routinely occurs behind the backs of the public. Information that is suppressed, voices that are not heard, views that are not aired, are silenced by the mechanisms of constituent censorship functioning though particular regulative techniques. (McGuigan 1996, p. 156)

In a non-democratic regime where freedom of speech is not promised, theoretically, the mechanisms of censorship are more direct and may be simpler to understand because they are explicitly exercised through state controlling mechanisms, usually authoritarian and maybe totalitarian (Sieber, Schramm and Patterson 1956). In authoritarian models, "The units of communication should support and advance the politics of the government in power so that this government can achieve its objectives" (p. 18). When they do so, censorship operates as an efficient, major regulatory tool of governing in authoritarian regimes:

> To the authoritarian, diversity of views is wasteful and irresponsible, dissent is an annoying nuisance and often subversive, and consensus and standardization are logical and sensible goals for mass communication. (Hatchten 1996, p. 15–16)

The totalitarian model is exemplified in communist regimes. It is the perfect authoritarian model (Saeys 2007, p. 62), strong enough to curb any hesitant diversity that may persist in weaker authoritarian settings. A totalitarian model describes the most restrictive forms of society, in which "all media belong to the state; all information and programming must serve the values and goals of a party-state and its totalitarian ideology" (Neveu 2004, p. 331).

Generally, however, there will be some degree of overlap between democratic and non-democratic regimes. This is evident, for example, in the case of contemporary China. As already discussed in earlier chapters, while little political freedom can be observed in China, economic liberalization has created the cultural freedom that Chinese consumers have long been craving. Furthermore, early signs of political liberalism are observable in Chinese cyberspace. Jayasuriya (2007) has described modern Chinese government as authoritarian liberalism. This may or may not be the case. However, importantly, the authoritarian–liberal label indicates that a regime is emerging from an authoritarian state where previously diversity and freedom barely existed. This is the case in China. This may be why current censorship mechanisms in contemporary China do not concern Chinese people as deeply as Western media coverage has assumed and expected.

The potential for structural change in China

Although previously rigorous censorship mechanisms in modern China have been loosened, this development does not necessarily indicate potential for structural changes in governance. Receiving increased freedoms of speech has made Chinese people more satisfied to live in the existing political regime. Both the general populace and the Chinese government are relatively content with present censorship practices, for example, which work subtly, depending on a combination of self-regulation and indirect state controls.

While China's political landscape has been gradually changing, there has been considerable attention to the nature and meaning of censorship in the West, in particular, its relationship to governance in China. But more important than how censorship is defined is how it is implemented.

I therefore reviewed censorship practices in China. I considered two historical periods, from the Song Dynasty to 1949, and, treating that year as a historical watershed, from 1949 to the market-oriented economic reforms period. This review demonstrated that historically Chinese people have long experience of tight censorship systems; no wonder they now appreciate the comparatively considerable freedom of speech they have recently been allowed. Finally, I contrasted the Chinese experience of censorship with models of a number of different types of regimes.

In sum, since the beginning of the twenty-first century, the Internet has empowered more people in more countries to participate in political events. This is true in China. In fact, China's experience of the Internet has attracted considerable attention from the West as a possible indicator of China's potential for democracy. So far, as I have argued, there is no evidence that the majority of Chinese people want, or are ready for, radical political changes, which are what a move to a democratic society would mean for China. Nonetheless, it is an important consideration, not least for China itself. in Chapter 5, I examine Western media's attention to censorship in China to try to answer the key question which concerns the West: Is the Internet giving rise to political change in China?

5

五

Chinese Anger with Western Media's Assumptions of Political Change

Political participation in China

Censorship mechanisms in China seem to have partially loosened up, affording Chinese people limited freedom to pursue personal goals. But will these apparent signs of political liberalism lead China to political democracy? This is the question that interests Western media. This chapter examines Western media interest in Chinese censorship so as to examine this key concern.

Although the Chinese government's encouragement of Internet use for personal consumption could be interpreted as an early symptom of political liberalism, in reality this encouragement has merely helped to stabilize the current political framework in China — witness Chinese bloggers' anger at Western criticisms of Chinese censorship practices (see Chapter 4). Analysis of the political implications of Internet use in China is crucial both to understanding Chinese bloggers' anger and to dissecting the short- and long-term potential for political change.

Chinese Internet use has attracted political interest and observation since it was first allowed, creating what Zhou has called a "monster complex" (2006, p. 2). During the global infancy of the Internet, Western observers tended to view it as a vehicle of expression and communication, a sort of benign monster that might lead authoritarian regimes to democracy. However, after witnessing the effective control of the Internet in China, the "benign monster" in China clearly proved to be less powerful than its rival, the Chinese government, and its effective censorship mechanisms. Subsequently, the Western media has credited the Chinese government as a powerful monster. Ever optimistic, though, Western media sources expected that the recent popularity of blogging in China might yet prove to be the benign monster that might defeat Chinese central controls. Clearly, though, this has not proven to be the case so far.

Contemporary research has moved far beyond making simple predictions about the relationship between freedom of expression and democracy in order to examine the dynamics and patterns of the social, cultural and political uses of new media technologies. Recent academic studies confirm the power of the benign monster in China. New technology has indeed empowered Chinese netizens to participate socially and politically. Despite the fact that the Internet filtering system in China is sophisticated (Zheng 2008), Yang (2009) argues that the Chinese government's control of the Internet has actually caused more resistance and subversion in cyberspace.

Certainly, the Internet in China has empowered political participation. Online social activism, as my research illustrates, has demonstrated that socio-political change is occurring in Chinese cyberspace. However, in this chapter I argue a different explanation from those suggested by Zheng and Yang: I argue that by allowing limited political discussion in Chinese cyberspace, the central government has actually stabilized Chinese society. It has done so by encouraging people to take responsibility for their consumer activities online. Indirectly, the government has created a contact point between the technologies of power and self: it has authorized self-regulation. Chinese people are simultaneously encouraged to be independent and to maintain control. Indirectly, the government is operating a censorship mechanism (see Foucault 1988a).

O'Donnell and Schmitter (1989) made a similar argument about the use of such strategies:

> Authoritarian rulers may tolerate or even promote liberalization in belief that by opening up certain spaces for individual and group action, they can relieve various pressures and obtain needed information and support without altering the structure of authority. (p. 9)

This chapter explores how this works in the case of present-day China.

Western media interest in Internet censorship in China

The question that first stimulated this study of Chinese bloggers' anger towards the Western critics of censorship issues in China was why did these issues attract the Western media's attention in the first place? I have suggested two possible reasons: the democratizing potential of the Internet in general, and the long-term potential of liberalization and control co-existing in the Chinese context. This section examines these two reasons.

The Internet: Its democratizing potential

The democratizing potential of the Internet has been predicted for at least a decade (Barber 1998; Grossman 1995) on the grounds that it might not only stimulate the break-up of dictatorships but also strengthen the freedoms in established democracies (Shapiro 1999). But although cyber libertarians believe the Internet will strengthen existing democracies or create new ones, sceptics have counter-argued that this technology might also reinforce surveillance procedures (Gandy 1993; Lyon 2003, p. 80). Consequently, due to the fast-growing Internet use in China, more research concerning the role of the Internet in facilitating democratization in China is of particular interest. Therefore, although there is no consensus on China's future as a political democracy, the Internet is generally considered a positive force for democracy (e.g. Barber 1998; Grossman 1995; Shapiro 1999; Zhou 2006).

Indeed, the early case of Mexico in the 1990s appears to confirm the Internet's democratizing potential (Castells 1997, p. 80), similarly, the more recent case of Indonesia, where the Internet was used to undermine authoritarian political control in the struggle to bring down the Suharto regime (Hill & Sen 2005). Not surprisingly, then, Internet censorship in China has become a popular topic in Western media coverage of China (e.g. the BBC and *The New York Daily*; see Appendix 1). With good reason, therefore, Western media sources watch the interplay in China between Internet users and the government in the hope of evidence of democratizing potential.

Liberalized central control: Its potential sustainability

That the Internet has had significant impacts on Chinese society has been widely observed. Reading online news, chatting online, searching for information, sending and receiving e-mails, playing online games — all are new habits for the Chinese, particularly young Chinese, who highly value being cyberspace consumers. In response, Chinese Internet enterprises such as QQ, Baidu, and Sohu are keen to encourage cyberspace consumerism. Nevertheless, the Internet has not brought democracy to China yet.

Chinese cyberspace operates in the mixed climate of authoritarianism and libertarianism, with the Chinese government sustaining a difficult, twofold strategy: encouraging liberalism on the Internet but minimizing the political risks to the government by maintaining control. These two strategies appear contradictory, because increasingly unimpeded use of the Internet necessitates decentralization, while the minimization of the political risks reinforces centralization (Zheng 2008, p. 49). Nonetheless, the current use of Chinese cyberspace has proved the compatibility of these two seemingly contradictory strategies as a unique feature of Chinese cyberspace. But on whether this compatibility in China is sustainable, the jury is still out. Hence the relevance of the following analysis of recent episodes of Chinese bloggers' anger at Western media's interest in censorship practices in China.

The time frame for my analysis is one year, from 2005 to 2006, the year when blogging was flourishing in China and when researchers on Internet practices in China became less optimistic about its liberalizing potential after witnessing the Chinese government's successful crackdowns.

Blogging is considered a powerful communication tool politically as well as socially. This is why Chinese Generation Y's extreme embrace of blogging has commanded Western media attention. Western journalists have participated in Chinese bloggers' conferences, browsed their blogs, and interviewed the writers behind the blogs. Although the Chinese government has constructed an extensive firewall to control the flow of information, that system has sufficient holes, so that the Chinese people have been able to experience at least some enjoyment from blogging (Anderson 2005). How long this equilibrium of partial or controlled freedom is sustainable is of considerable interest to researchers, politicians and journalists, even though it is a question that currently remains unanswered.

Internet censorship mechanisms

Internet censorship is a global concept. The censorship mechanism in Chinese cyberspace is one of the most sophisticated in the world. Global empirical analysis of Internet filtering has been conducted for some years, mainly by two organizations: Electronic Frontiers Australia (EFA) and the Open Net Initiative (ONI). The EFA was established in 1994 to protect and promote civil liberties via the Internet and, where necessary, to advocate the amendment of laws and regulations to ensure these liberties. Since its last report in 2002 on global Internet censorship, the EFA has concentrated on Australia. The ONI, founded in 2003, is a collaborative partnership among four leading academic institutions: the Citizen Lab at the Munk Centre for International Studies, University of Toronto; the Berkman Center for Internet and Society at Harvard Law School; the Advanced Network Research Group at the Cambridge Security Programme (Centre for International Studies) at the University of Cambridge, and; the Oxford Internet Institute at the University of Oxford, which joined later than the other three (Deibert et al. 2008). On the basis of the ONI's most recent publication, which is "the first systematic, academically rigorous global study of all known state-mandated Internet filtering practices" (Zittrain & Palfrey 2008, in Deibert et al. 2008, p. 3), combined with the ONI's latest updates on their website (opennet.net), I here present a brief overview of Internet filtering around the world focusing on four regions — Asia, the United States and Canada, Europe, and Australia and New Zealand — in order to provide a ground for contrast with the context of China.

Internet censorship in Asia is more complicated than in other regions of the world. Of the eleven countries the ONI tested in this region, China, Burma, and Vietnam had the most complicated Internet filter mechanisms. Blocked contents ranged from human rights issues, to reform and opposition activities, to conflict and security materials. In contrast, less social content was blocked in Asia. Apart from pornographic content, which is commonly blocked across Asia, Pakistan and India blocked some religious materials, and South Korea and Thailand blocked a small portion of gambling material.

In the US and Canada, state-mandated filtering has not been found, but the Internet is not totally unfettered in either country (Goldsmith & Wu 2006, p. 65–84). From legislation to technical regulation, Internet censorship in these two countries mainly operates in four areas: child protection, national security, computer security, and intellectual property. Apart from the area of child pornography, most censorship in the US and Canada occurs after publication, and most censorship is the result of private rather than government action.

In Europe, the implementation of Internet censorship has been dramatic. From envisaging the Internet as a democratic tool enabling freedom of expression, since the beginning of the twenty-first century most European countries have filtered the Internet in a variety of forms. These mainly include the blocking of child pornography and racism, as well as materials that incite hatred and terrorism (Deibert et al. 2008, p. 203). However, this filtering is termed voluntary rather than mandatory, and mostly occurs elsewhere in Western democratic countries such as Australia.

Australia possesses no explicit protection of freedom of speech in its constitution (Jordan 2002). It remains the most restrictive Internet filtering country among Western nations. With the government's plans of ISP level filtering in 2009, Australia became the first Western democracy to push mandatory Internet filtering. By contrast, Australia's neighbour New Zealand is much softer on Internet regulation, its definition of offensive contents being much more limited than that of Australia.

China's Internet censorship mechanisms

China is famous not only for its Great Wall but also for its great firewall. According to the ONI, China has one of the largest and most sophisticated filtering systems. With a focus on the Chinese government's tactical exercise of power, this section examines Chinese Internet censorship using the framework constructed in the previous chapter (see Table 4.1). I point out that self-censorship (an example of Foucault's concept of technologies of the self) has emerged as the dominant mechanism in Chinese cyberspace, although direct control mechanisms remain on standby.

Forms of imposed censorship

Internet censorship mechanisms in China have demonstrated both defensive and offensive characteristics, which involve removal and replacement strategies to prevent information from reaching the public as well as displacement and dispersal strategies that disseminate a particular version of public information so as to drown out other less desirable perspectives. Whereas in defensive censorship a government or organization filters undesirable information, in offensive censorship it allows only desirable information. Defensive censorship predominates in Chinese cyberspace; the widely circulated list of banned words in Chinese cyberspace tells us there are more than 1,000 taboo terms (Xiao 2004; Pan 2006; Weiquan Wang 2008).

Meanwhile, offensive censorship is often applied to unpredictable, significant but negative incidents on which information cannot be simply blocked. In such instances, offensive censorship complements defensive censorship. For example, in both the case of the SARS disease in 2003 and that of poisoned milk powder in 2008 when government officials could not prevent some information about these catastrophes reaching at least some sections of the general populace, they made positive, optimistic public announcements early on (BBC 2008).

While deliberate censorship screens out materials that are against the Chinese government's censorship laws and regulations, another form of censorship, structural censorship, operates through China's market economy. Structural censorship particularly affects foreign enterprises that do business in China. From Fortune 500 companies to Google, Yahoo!, Skype and Websense — indeed all such foreign companies in China whose dominant aim is commercial profit — in effect, help the Chinese government to censor and restrict Chinese Internet consumers. Foreign companies, however, deny having signed any explicit contract with the Chinese central government. Instead they state that blocking occurs in China and who and what is blocked is beyond their control (Hu 2002). For example, when Microsoft responded to the human rights organization Amnesty International, which has as one of its aims to improve freedom of expression worldwide, it asserted that it was "focused on delivering the best technology to people throughout the world" (Hu 2002). Delivery of e-technology is one thing; how its use is controlled, however, is another. According to Amnesty International, China continued to arrest Internet activists who overtly breached Internet laws between 1998 and 2008. In 2008, for instance, Chinese police arrested 28 suspects in the name of cracking down on Internet pornography. This action was direct censorship and evidence of Foucault's technology of power operating when the technology of self wasn't implemented — when, in other words, there was no contact point between the two kinds of technologies.

While direct, structural censorship is a top-down operation carried out by the government and its agents who exercise sovereign power, subtle censorship, although structural, largely involves technologies of the self, that is, forms of self-censorship. Increasingly it is noticeable that the Chinese government has broadened its approach to include fostering indirect, subtler strategies such as corporate self-censorship and spin in addition to its more blatant forms of suppression such as firewall blocking (MacKinnon 2009b).

Forms of self-censorship

The promotion of self-censorship among individuals and domestic-content Internet providers in China has been evident for nearly a decade (Hachigian 2001). In Chinese cyberspace, the institutionalized mechanism for formal self-censorship is realized through commitment to the "Public Pledge of Self-Regulation and Professional Ethics for China's Internet Industry" issued by the Internal Society of China (Klang & Murray 2005, pp. 11–26). Since 2002, more than 100 Internet businesses in China have signed the public pledge and adopted self-censorship by banning information they believe will be deemed undesirable (Frontline 2003).

At organizational and individual levels, self-censorship is practised intentionally when it is implemented through intricate surveillance mechanisms. But it has also been assimilated unintentionally since getting rich first before any other achievements is the motto shared by Chinese society (Klang & Murray 2005, p. 115). In other words, self-censorship in China today is not only fear-driven but also money-driven. For mainstream Internet users in China today, their online behaviours are shaped through their increasing reliance on consumerism and the government's ultimate aim to produce self-regulating consumers. However, it is important to notice also that, whilst previously Chinese netizens usually self-censored their postings on political topics, Chinese cyberspace now displays a wider range of acceptable issues. Political topics including sensitive keywords such as "Tibet", which were previously censored, are no longer taboo in Chinese cyberspace. To illustrate the change, I provide contrasting examples, first, in 2004 and, second, in 2009.

In 2004, on the last day of the Taiwanese presidential elections, Chen Shuibian, one of the presidential candidates, together with his running mate Lv Xiulian, were shot and injured. One would expect that online news platforms or discussion boards in China would have covered this topic. However, not only did the news platforms remain silent on this issue but so also did chat rooms and discussion boards, except for a few comments on the *People's Daily* Strong Country Forum [*Qiangguo Luntan*] and the official website of the Xinhua News Agency. The silence in Chinese cyberspace on this topic, which was of considerable interest to

Chinese people, was most likely due to its being sensitive "Taiwan Straits politics" (Lagerkvist 2006, p. 43).

In contrast, on 28 March 2009, the day marking what Western media called "China's 50 years of control over Tibet" and which Chinese media claimed to be the "50 years of democratic reform in Tibet", one would expect Chinese netizens to have maintained silence as they did five years previously on the Taiwan election shootings, because Tibet is a topic as sensitive as Taiwan Straits politics. However, almost all online news platforms, from propaganda machines such as China's Central TV station's website to more sensational and entertaining websites such as QQ news, reported on this important day in Chinese history (see Appendix 2). Also, on the aforementioned platform the *People's Daily* Strong Country Forum [*Qiangguo Luntan*], there were more than 70 topics posted on Tibet that day among a total of 5,000 Tibetan topics posted before and after the day. However, most of the comments celebrated this anniversary day as one that honoured the liberation of Tibetan serfs by the Chinese Communist Party 50 years earlier (see Appendix 3).

These two examples indicate a modicum of change in the practice of self-censorship in China: while political topics were rarely discussed in 2004 in the Strong Country Forum, they were allowed for discussion in 2008 in the same forum, albeit with a dominant pro-China perspective. Although political participation and online activism occur in Chinese cyberspace, they do so, then, when they fit the intentions of the central Chinese government, as the following sections in this chapter demonstrate. Chinese Internet censorship is still the most sophisticated in the world. The government adopts all forms of censorship — direct, indirect, structured, subtle and self-regulated — and the strategies employed embrace the exercise of power from top down to bottom up. Although, as I have suggested, there have been some indications of moderate relaxation in the implementation of censorship (for example, some discussion of sensitive political issues is currently allowed such as on the relationship between Tibet and China), the opening-up still operates within a restricted discursive framework. But whether such relaxations are politically liberalizing in that they will lead to changes in the structure of authority in China, is the main issue examined in the next two chapter sections.

Chinese cyberspace usage: Its political implications

Liberalizing personal Internet use

This section, drawing on illustrations of Chinese cyberspace use, investigates the political implications of liberalizing personal Internet use. Consumer culture dominates social behaviour in current China, astonishingly so in China's cyberspace. While Chinese usage of the Internet is expanding generally, the biggest increase in Internet use is undoubtedly consumerist oriented. Look, for example, at the top two most popular discussion boards in Chinese cyberspace, the Baidu post bar (http://post.baidu.com) and QQ forum (http://bbs.qq.com), and it is not hard to see the largely consumerist-empowered ideology. In Baidu post bar, the catalogue is composed of 19 main subtitles (see Figure 5.1) that translate as follows: celebrities, sports, music, cartoon, emotion, science and culture, literature and arts, making local friends, personal spaces, computer and digital, movies and TV dramas, fashion and leisure, TV programs, games, business, campus, stock and fund, Baidu post family members, Baidu post family friends. These contents reflect one overarching theme: consumerism.

According to a 2009 statistical survey, QQ has 860 million registered accounts, it has more users than Facebook, and it is the most popular communication tool in Chinese cyberspace (people.com.cn 2009). The QQ forum also mirrors the largely consumerist orientation of Chinese cyberspace. The QQ catalogue has 17 subtitles: forum services, entertainment, finance, sports, radio, games, fashion, technology, cartoon, childcare, cars, women, education, astrology, world exposition, news, and ideology. The popularity of each topic demonstrates extreme unevenness between consumerism and other interests. While three sections — cars, entertainment and games — have more than 120 sub-sections (see Figure 5.2), news and ideology have only four and six sub-sections respectively (see Figure 5.3).

In short, government empowerment of consumer culture has achieved what it set out to do: the government has created "free" cyberspace for Chinese Internet users to pursue their personal desires as consumers.

Sexual content

Apart from being liberalized as consumers, Chinese netizens now have some autonomy to explore sexual topics in Chinese cyberspace. Similar to many other Asian countries, China's Internet laws clearly state that *porn* and *lewd* content are not allowed in cyberspace (Deibert et al. 2008). However, the censorship of obscene materials in Chinese cyberspace is *ad hoc*. In China, where people's political views are blocked, Chinese netizens enjoy considerable freedom to explore sexual matters in comparison with netizens in other Asian countries where sexual content is filtered.

The government first started to curb the availability of porn and lewd content in August 2004 with an official announcement launching a special operation to crack down on online porn and lewd content through legislation (Chinalaw.gov.cn 2004). This crackdown was in response to liberalization on sexual issues that had already taken place. Three to four new porn websites had been emerging every day since 2001 (Sina News 2004). The first crackdown was mainly ignited by the world-known breach of restrictions on sexual material and nudity in December 2003 by Chinese blogger Mu Zi Mei. Her blog contained explicit descriptions of her one-night stands with various men. This was the first case of such explicit sexual content being posted in Chinese cyberspace. However, when the crackdown paused in 2005, the porn and obscene content flooded back to Chinese cyberspace, and even reached minors. In 2007, China undertook its second major crackdown, which lasted for six months and shut down 3,614 porn websites (China.com.cn 2007). The third large crackdown commenced in January 2008 and lasted until August the same year. According to the *People's Daily* in February 2009, more than 1,900 websites were shut down because they had pornographic and lewd postings during that time (*People's Daily* 2009).

The general pattern of response to crackdown filtering of obscene information in Chinese cyberspace is that porn and lewd content resurges quickly and turbulently once the crackdown campaign stops; meanwhile, sex website providers tend to breach the government's

Figure 5.1: The catalogue of Baidu post bar
Source: http://tieba.baidu.com/ (accessed 12 June 2010)

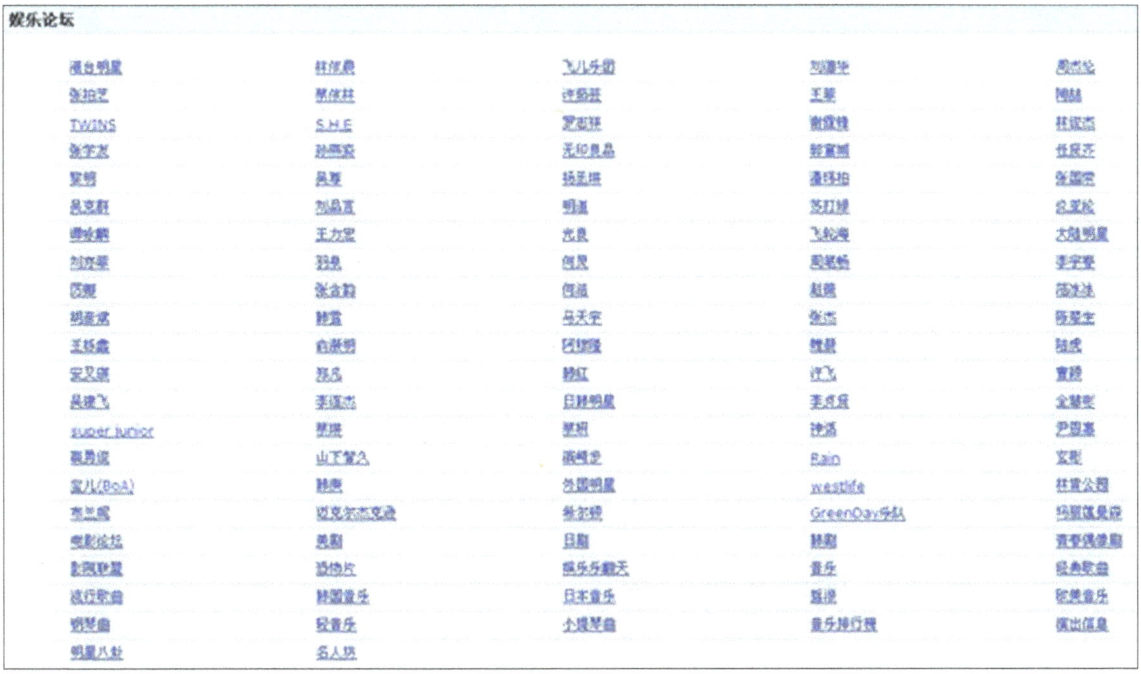

Figure 5.2: Sub-section under "Entertainment" on QQ Forum
Source: http://bbs.qq.com/ (accessed 23 June 2010)

Figure 5.3: Sub-section under "News" and "Ideology" on QQ Forum
Source: http://bbs.qq.com/ (accessed 23 June 2010)

Figure 5.4: Contradiction between prohibition and the listing "Porn Videos" on China's sexual websites
Source: http://bbs.sexkang.net/ (accessed 25 June 2010)

restrictions on porn and lewd content. Take one of the popular sex websites in China, "sexkang. net", for example: although the discussion forum clearly states "Porn and lewd materials are prohibited in this Forum", explicit porn videos are indicated in the topics not far from the solemn statement (see Figure 5.4).

Cyberspace has also provided a platform for offline sexual relationships in China and so facilitates the "sexual revolution silently going on in China" (*China Daily* 2005). According to this domestic survey in China, 46 per cent of the more than 20,000 pregnant teenage girls in Shanghai said they had had sexual relationship with boys they met online. Chinese media have observed that China's one-night-stand rate has soared along with the numbers of China's Internet users (Yahoo 2007). Furthermore, Chinese cyberspace is also more tolerant on homosexual issues. The Chinese Internet search engine Baidu contains more than 12,500,000 topics on homosexuality, including videos (see Appendix 4). Chinese gay websites such as "boysky.com", "boysky.org" and "iboysky.com" have both Chinese and English versions and provide services from online video chatting and discussion forums to blogging for the national gay community. According to statistics cited on these websites, China's gay population now numbers more than 50 million (iboysky.com 2009).

Thus, free expression is now clearly tolerated in a topic area Chinese people used to shy away from. In other words, Chinese Internet users have been allowed another area in which to pursue their personal desires.

Political freedoms in Chinese cyberspace

Increasing freedoms of expression in China relate to more than consumerism and sexuality, however. They are tentatively expanding into political areas, still under tight control as recently as a decade ago. These political freedoms of expression in China can be categorized in three groups: critical with "correct" political ideologies, critical with "incorrect" political ideologies, and praising the party. Since the freedom to post materials praising the party is not an indicator of political liberalization, I review and illustrate only the first two categories below.

Critical with "correct" political ideologies

On 1 October 2003, Li Xin De, who is one of China's foremost public opinion watchers, founded the first and now most famous anti-corruption website, the "China public opinion watching website" (www.cnyulun.com). Soon after its founding in 2003, the site unveiled the corruption of the Deputy Mayor of Ji Ning city in Shan Dong province and 46 days later the Deputy Mayor was arrested. This incident is considered a milestone in the history of Chinese netizens' political participation (Zhang 2009). Since 2003, Chinese netizens have felt encouraged to participate in political matters, having a noticeable impact on the government's decision making in some cases, including: the online campaign in 2007 of Chinese bloggers to fight the proposed building of a harmful chemical factory in Shenzhen (Cody 2007); the tracking down in 2008 of a government official involved in a sexual harassment incident (Sina News 2008), and; the formal assistance of bloggers in 2009 in a local government's investigation of a prisoner's strange death (Sina News 2009, 28/09). From the Strong Nation Forum, the most famous political discussion board, to Tianya BBS, a more sensational space dominated by celebrity gossips and online game discussions, Chinese netizens are uncovering corrupt officials, commenting on current affairs, making suggestions about unpopular government policies and even discussing "sensitive topics".

Figure 5.5: Topics from gznf.net/forum on 1 April 2009
Source: http://www.gznf.net/forum/forum-7-1.html (accessed 12 July 2010)

Figure 5.6: Comments on the one topic of "cultural revolution" on Strong Nation Forum
Source: http://bbs1.people.com.cn/postDetail.do?view=1&id=91402204&bid=1 (accessed 15 July 2010)

年进入四月十五号,我们就会被一种情绪笼罩,越接近六月,这种情绪越强烈。我们需要跟有同样的"钟"的朋友们一同悼念排解悲伤。六四屠杀后,全国处于白色恐怖当中,我和家人朋友尚且关起门点燃蜡烛哀悼死难者,我从来没有想过:十九年后,在一个自由的社会里悼念手无寸铁的被杀害的平民百姓还需要理由。 可是,今年的纪念活动,从主办单位给记者招待会开始,就被问到地震后举办六四纪念活动是否合适。从筹办到活动的整个过程当中,主办方在不同场合要不断解释:有没有给地震灾民捐款,捐了多少;解释这次地震的伤亡不只是天灾,还是人祸;解释19年前的反腐败诉求与豆腐渣教学楼是有联系的;解释我们反对的是中共政府而不是中国人民,解释就算是二十年的所谓稳定也不应该以人命为代价。曾几何时,国人不再把杀人看成罪恶,而悼念死难者却需要理由。倘若人们真地需要一个悼念六四死难者的理由,我会列出L的89见证: "我在广场的救护站中醒过来。医生和护理员我知道我是香港的学生,虽然明知我并无大碍,仍坚持送我到医院。我身边躺着一个浑身鲜血的学生。他的脊背血肉模糊,身体已不能动弹,但仍不停地说:"要坚持到底!要坚持到底!"第一辆救护车来到时,我没有上,第二辆,我仍然挣扎着不着上。一位女医生握着我的手,哭着用英语跟我说,"你一定要平安回到香港,让全世界知道这里发生的事,知道吗!" 杀

人灭口十九年 一九八九年六月四号前后在中国发生的事情后来全世界都知道了,但大部分的国人却不知道;世界各国的青年人都可以了解,唯独中国的新一代不了解。要是说屠夫们在1989年杀了人,那么他们在过去的十九年就在灭口;为了灭口接着杀人,然后再灭口。 为了灭口,他们不让中国人民大学的死难者吴国峰的父母把儿子的遗体运回四川老家,他们把他右胸、肩膀、肋骨和手臂都中枪,肚子被刺刀刺了七八公分长连肠子都拉出来的尸体强行火化; 为了灭口,他们强迫全民表态,把天安门广场变成秘密警察广场; 为了灭口,他们非法没收国际社会给天安门难属的人道援助汇款,死难者王建平的双胞胎女儿到了十五岁才因为奶奶收到的人道捐款而第一次在家里看上电视; 为了灭口,他们长期监听、监视、迫害要求给受难者讨回公道的天安门母亲群体,母亲们在悲伤恐惧与愤怒中度过余生; 为了灭口,他们软禁前总理赵紫阳,通死号报编辑钦本立,监禁为共产党坐过国民党大牢的王若望,中伤支持民主理念的方励之,拒绝屠城见证人汉学家林培瑞入境; 为了灭口,他们把刽子手封为"共和国勇士",把"爱国主义教育"变成爱党主义教育,把反右文革六四的真相一笔勾销; 十九年的杀人灭口与红色洗脑之后,他们不再需要象对付喻华峰程中益李大同那样去对付敢言的长平 "爱国"愤青自然会群起而攻之; 十九年的杀人灭口与红色洗脑之后,他们不再需要动用机枪坦克去镇压学生抗议,因为抗议者只反日反美反CNN,但不反共不反中央电视台不反人民日报; 十九年的杀人灭口与红色洗脑之后,"爱国者"学会了什么时候需要挥红旗的热血,什么时候需要视而不见的沉默。他们满腔热血地去唱"家乐福",去监督批评别人的地震捐款数目,但却漠视山西黑砖窑里的奴工,漠视河南艾滋病村里农家的新坟旧墓,漠视来自凉山的幼奴,漠视因"让领导先走"而葬身火海的孩子们,漠视在绝望中含去死去的天安门母亲。 与杀人灭口和红色洗脑"不和谐"的异议声音和民间的维权力量最后都要面对象对胡佳式的软禁绑架;对李方平式的毒打;对艾晓明式的威胁;对廖亦武式的剥夺出国权利;或者干脆象陈光诚、郭飞雄那样变成监牢里的犯人代号。没有人会在乎他们是为了太石村那些土地被强抢的村民讨公道; 为了临沂县那些没有结婚被迫作绝育手术的妇女讨公道; 为了那些因为贫穷

Translation:

The whole world knows about what happened on 4th June in 1989 except most Chinese mainlanders; all the young generation in the world can understand except China's young generation who don't understand. If I say butchers killed people in 1989, then they have been destroying people in the last 19 years… After 19 years of extermination and red brainwashing, they don't need guns and tanks to suppress students' protests, because protesters nowadays are only anti-Japan, anti-American, anti-CNN, not anti-CCP, anti-Chinese Central TV station, anti-People's Daily; after 19 years of suppression and red brainwashing, patriots learned when to donate their blood, when to keep silent. They boycott "Carrefour" passionately, they criticize others' earthquake donations, but they turn a blind eye towards the mining slaves in Shanxi province…

Figure 5.7: MSN blog entry 25 July 2008: "19 years massacre: From white terror to red terror"
Source: http://cid-7b0a9f258b67c8f1.spaces.live.com/blog/cns!7B0A9F258B67C8F1!153.entry (accessed 16 July 2010)

Translation:

… Mocking civilians around will get harder and harder. The dictators' wishful thinking will not last for long. As long as Chinese people have confidence, trust themselves and their fellow citizens, the trend of democratizing will be unstoppable; the day citizens govern the country will arrive one day.

Figure 5.8: Sina blog entry 21 January 2009: "The created theory of anti-democracy in China"
Source: http://blog.sina.com.cn/s/blog_53597d320100bzm1.html (accessed 18 July 2009)

For example, on a local online discussion forum of Guangzhou city in Pearl River delta, topics vary from exposing local government corruption to criticizing China's one-child policy (see Figure 5.5).

Sensitive keywords that once were forbidden in Chinese cyberspace are now discussable. For example, the hot topics of the month in Strong Nation Forum in March 2009 included a post titled "Passionate Images of the Cultural Revolution". It contained the sensitive keywords "cultural revolution" and images of the Cultural Revolution period that demonstrate how passionate people were during that time. While most comments praised Chairman Mao, comments such as "It was a nightmare" and "A history of absurdity" did appear. But there were no comments relating this issue to the current Communist Party (see Figure 5.6). "Correct" political ideology is the dominant feature of political discussions in Chinese cyberspace.

This feature picks up the argument in Chapter 3, namely, that promoting consumerism also fosters nationalism in current China in ways that benefit the central government. Regular postings on anti-corruption topics demonstrate netizens' awareness of current social problems in China. These concerns have given birth to online vigilantes in China who seek out offline wrongdoers. However, their actions tend to lead to a "cyber-mob" mentality whereby such vigilantes link their push for anti-corruption measures to their strong belief that those who are able to act corruptly do so at the expense of the rest of the population (Ford 2008). And while this phenomenon promotes the consumerist culture and stimulates a shared interest between netizens and government in corruption on a national scale, at the same time it distracts online consumers' attention from continuing domestic problems.

Critical with "incorrect" political ideologies

In the political areas discussed above, the topics may include sensitive words, but few of the discussions are negative about the central government and Chinese Communist Party. However, some anti-government comments do appear in Chinese cyberspace. For example, on the MSN website, a blog entry accuses the Chinese Communist Party of a massacre in 1989 and brainwashing tactics with the new generation (see Figure 5.7).

Also, in Sina blog, a Chinese blogger claims current Chinese communist party members are dictators and suggests the move to democracy will be unstoppable as long as Chinese citizens have confidence (see Figure 5.8).

To conclude that the controlling strategies in Chinese cyberspace are not undergoing some changes would be overly pessimistic. However, to conclude that political liberalism is increasing in Chinese cyberspace might be overly optimistic. In the next section, I discuss how these pockets of liberalism should be understood in relation to concurrent changes in the government's controlling strategies. The discussion takes off from a definition of liberalization offered by O'Donnell & Schmitter (1986), who base their own understanding on an analysis of contemporary scholarship.

The potential for political change

Only early stages of liberalization

> [Liberalization is the] process of making effective certain rights that protect both individuals and social groups from arbitrary or illegal acts committed by the state or third parties. On the level of individuals, these guarantees include the classical elements of the liberal tradition: habeas corpus; sanctity of private home and correspondence; the right to be defended in a fair trial according to pre-established laws; freedom of movement, speech, and petition; and so forth. On the level of groups, these rights cover such things as freedom from punishment for expressions of collective dissent from government policy, freedom from censorship of the means of communication, and freedom to associate voluntarily with other citizens. (O'Donnell & Schmitter 1986, p. 7)

Locating the online political landscape in China in the context of O'Donnell and Schmitter's framework for liberalization above, I argue that use of the Internet in China indicates some early stages of political liberalization. Individuals communicating in China's cyberspace do post petitions, accuse local government officials of corruption and seek to protect their rights according to established laws. For example, on gznf.net/forum (2009) netizens posted "A public letter to People's Congress Representatives", "Local government is so corrupt, where is the law?!", and "The Director of Urban Administrative Office is cruel and corrupt!" (see Figure 5.5).

There have also been cases of groups expressing collective dissent from government policy and remaining unpunished and free to associate with other citizens as they chose. For example, in the 2007 campaign against the government's decision to build a chemical factory in Xiamen, protesters had the freedom to spread the information online and protest offline. Not only were they not punished, but they successfully influenced the government to build the factory at another place. The case of this campaign is important to the argument in this section. Hence, an overview of the 2007 anti-factory campaign follows.

In 2007, the Chinese government planned to build a 300-acre, $1.4 billion chemical factory in Xiamen, Southeast China. The chemical products proposed were known to cause eye, ear, nose and throat irritations and damage the nervous system (*The Standard* 2007). When Chemistry Professor Zhao at Xiamen University found out about the potential threats to the local community posed by the building of this factory, she organized a petition of 100 other signatories against the building plan (EastSouthWestNorth 2007). Zhao's petition was based on an explosion at a chemical factory in Northern China in 2005, which had released toxic chemicals into the Songhua River contaminating the water supply in the major city of Harbin. Zhao submitted her petition not only to the local officials but also to the National Development and Reform Commission in Beijing. However, since the growth of GDP is the priority on the government's agenda, the government approved the plan to build this factory (*The Standard* 2007).

A blogger known as Lian Yue stepped in. He used his blog on Bullog.cn to circulate Professor Zhao's questions among the Xiamen public (EastSouthWestNorth 2007) because the local newspapers and television news were disseminating only positive aspects of the plan. After Lian Yue and other Internet commentators raised the potential threats posed by this factory, reporters from national magazines started arriving in Xiamen to interview Lian Yue and report on the local residents' protests (The Standard 2007). Another blogger, Zoula, sent live updates on the local residents' demonstrations from his mobile phone to his blog (Kennedy 2007). Local residents mobilized quickly when they heard that the factory threatened the environment. President Hu Jintao paid attention to the protests and, on May 29, government officials agreed to review the plan of the factory originally approved in 2005. A delay in building was agreed and it was later confirmed that the factory would be built at another place (Zaobao.com 2008a).

The 2007 anti-factory campaign is a clear demonstration of collective dissent free from Chinese government intervention (see the epigraph to this section). But it is impossible to conclude that these signs of early stages of liberalization will lead China to democracy. For China to move from these early stages to further levels of liberalization, the existing episodes of liberal behaviour would have to be replicated and accumulate in ways that institutionalize such liberal practices, so that people see that exercising free rights will continue to go unpunished and so "dare to do the same" (O'Donnell & Schmitter 1986, p. 7). The early stages of liberalization are fraught by their dependence upon government approval, which is likely to be unreliable and inconsistent.

Based on how the Chinese government exercises power — especially its implementation of the censorship mechanisms on the Internet analyzed earlier in this chapter — it is safe to say the exercise of governmental power in China remains inconsistent, "arbitrary and capricious" (O'Donnell & Schmitter 1986, p. 7). Cases such as those examined in this chapter that have displayed evidence of early stages of political liberalization in Chinese cyberspace are also subject to a crucial factor that will determine whether China will proceed to liberalize further: namely, the liberalized practices identified are not likely to accumulate, meaning that any other cases of political liberalization are equally likely to remain isolated. I will strengthen this point through some examples.

Take the two cases of politically "incorrect" ideologies already mentioned (see Figures 5.7 and 5.8). Although China has nearly 300 million Internet users, the Sina blog entry on "dictators and the future of China democracy" has only 51 readers with 5 comments (Figure 5.8). The other blog entry on the "1989 massacre" is even more unpopular (Figure 5.7); it has had hardly any visitors apart from me. This phenomenon can be explained by remembering the demographics of Internet users in China. It is not hard to tell the posts with "incorrect" political views are written by the older generations in China from the way they are written. On the other hand, mainstream Internet users — nearly 70 per cent of the 300 million netizens are under 30 years old — are not likely to post the same views as the older generation. They tend to dislike the "incorrect" political views. Because they, China's generation Y, have experienced a peaceful China and comfortable life, they are far more interested in enjoying their personal freedom than getting involved in politics. As a pop song in Chinese cyberspace goes:

No Communist Party, no new China;

No new China, no new life;

No new life, no sexual life;

No sexual life, how can I survive?! (Baidu 2008)

The Chinese blogosphere case study in Chapter 6 further illustrates Chinese Generation Y's preference for pursuing personal rather than political freedom.

The seemingly arbitrary, capricious exercise of governmental power in China manipulates this preference and political loyalty, working in diverse ways and with careful timing to prevent incidents building up in ways that could threaten the regime. In the case of the 2007 campaign organized largely by the successful dissemination of information by videos on blogs against the government's plan to build a chemical factory in Xiamen, although unsanctioned protests had a noticeable influence on the government's decision making, there were other subsequent actions. First, the government shut down the blog service provider of Lian Yue's blog. Second, in the last few days of 2007, two government ministries, China's State Administration of Radio, Film and Television (SARFT) and Ministry of Information

Industry (MII), co-published the new Regulations for Online Audio and Video Services. These took effect from 31January 2008 (Marbridge Daily 2007) and included the following regulation: "unlicensed companies are not allowed to provide audio and video upload services for individuals, and even licensed companies may not allow individuals to upload news content" (chinasarft.gov.cn 2007).

Democracy remains a distant prospect

> Authoritarian rulers may tolerate or even promote liberalization in belief that by opening up certain spaces for individual and group action, they can relieve various pressures and obtain needed information and support without altering the structure of authority, that is, without becoming accountable to the citizenry for their actions or subjecting their claim to rule to fair and competitive elections. (O'Donnell and Schmitter 1986, p. 9)

Chinese authorities, while allowing some individuals and some groups to influence government decision-making in isolated episodes, have not moved to encourage systematic participation of the general population in political processes. There has been no spread and accumulation of liberalization, no institutionalization of liberal practices — the conditions O'Donnell and Schmitter (1986) identified as essential for liberalization to lead to democratization. Without structural changes that weaken centralized political control, there is no opportunity to change existing political systems (Zheng 2008, p. 88). In other words, democratization requires structural change, whereas liberalization can take place within an existing political framework. That is how authoritarian regimes can tolerate limited signs of political liberalization — and may even be encouraged as a means of maintaining people's loyalty.

I argue, therefore, that in the case of China opportunities to discuss political matters have been limited in order to legitimate and stabilize the existing political framework. However, other tactics control this political freedom. For example, the government stimulates nationalist sentiment by encouraging consumerism in Chinese cyberspace. Shaping Chinese netizens' core identities as consumers, rather than citizens, is the ultimate goal of the Chinese government. In Foucault's terms, creating limited so-called free political spaces enables people to develop technologies of self which can be controlled, if necessary, subtly and indirectly — to the extent that individuals will see codes or rules as representations or technologies of truth (1983, p. 214).

Political stability

This chapter has examined the fundamental question "Is the Internet bringing political change in China?" It has considered current Internet censorship practices in China and analyzed the limited freedoms allowed in Chinese cyberspace. It found that limited liberalism legitimates and stabilizes the existing political framework in China through shaping Chinese Internet users as consumers rather than citizens.

The limited freedoms of political expression afforded people in Chinese cyberspace possibly mark the beginning of wider political freedoms. However, to predict that these tentative signs in cyberspace will lead to wholesale political democratization is a misrepresentation of reality. The government has in part created the environment for current political freedoms, and is deliberately allowing limited degrees of personal autonomy as an indirect means of maintaining people's loyalty to the state. The Chinese people, particularly the young generation, have been ready to accept this balance of freedom and power because they acknowledge that they have considerably more freedoms than earlier generations. That is why the Chinese government has not needed direct Internet censorship when Western media have criticized China's human rights practices. Rather than agreeing, Chinese bloggers have perceived such criticism as an attack on China's reputation. In all the examples discussed in this book, Chinese netizens have been quick to defend China's actions. Therefore, Chinese bloggers do not experience existing Internet censorship strategies as problematic and nationalist discourse remains a feature of their responses to the unpopular Western focus on censorship issues in China.

In sum, the analyses of Chapters 3, 4 and 5 suggest the structural changes required for democratization are unlikely to happen in present-day China for three main reasons:

1. The government has stimulated national loyalty in Generation Y by encouraging its increasing interest in consumerism.
2. Western and Chinese people have different experiences and understandings of how censorship practices affect political sentiment in China, with the majority of China's Generation Y not feeling threatened by political censorship because they have gained personal freedom not previously allowed.
3. General Western assumptions about the political implications of the Internet in China are not borne out by the political realities.

Because the differences in understanding between the West and China on censorship and its implications for freedom and democracy are so marked, Chapter 6 provides a detailed examination of a blogging incident that attracted considerable international attention and was one of the original stimuli for this book. The case analysis provides strong support for the argument mounted in the previous chapters.

PART III

Stabilizing China's Polity

6

Nationalism as a Consumer-Oriented Product

In Chapter 2 I examined the Chinese blogging community as a case of Chinese government encouragement of consumerist culture in order to stimulate nationalism. In this chapter, I focus on one blogging phenomenon in particular, the Anti-CNN website established in the Chinese blogosphere, in order to portray how the Chinese government also regulates nationalism to prevent it from getting out of control. I argue that although party propaganda does not cause the nationalist sentiments of Chinese bloggers, as is the dominant perception in the West, those sentiments are, as suggested recently (Fong 2004; Zhao 2002; Zhou 2005), not free from Chinese state intervention. Drawing on the explanations offered in Part II of this book, together with an analysis of samples collected from the Anti-CNN forum, this chapter argues that instead of using a direct tool such as propaganda, the Chinese government shapes bloggers' nationalist sentiments by encouraging their reliance on consumer culture.

A rational approach to nationalism

The Anti-CNN episode

On 18 March 2008, a 23-year-old male Chinese graduate from Tsinghua University registered the domain name "anti-cnn.com" in response to what he perceived as biased Western coverage of the Tibetan unrest. He followed this with the registration of a series of domain names such as "anti-bbc.com", "anti-voa.com", "anti-spiegel.com", "anti-ntv.com", and "anti-rtl.com". Two days later, on 20 March, the website "anti-cnn.com" was activated, going online with a headline on its homepage: "The truth of Tibet: full documentation of how the Western media slanders China". As the website indicated, Anti-CNN did not only object to the American company CNN, but also to many other Western media agencies, such as the BBC, *Der Spiegel*, *La Repubblica*, n-tv, *Bild*, Fox News Channel and RTL (Wikipedia Contributors 2009). The website stated, "We are not against the western media, but against the lies and fabricated stories in the media. We are not against western people, but against the prejudice in western society"

(Anti-CNN 2008c). Meanwhile, the Anti-CNN website publicized its e-mail address, calling on Chinese netizens to collect what the website called "the evidences of Western media's 'evil behaviours'" and send them to Anti-CNN's e-mail account. Domestic Chinese websites and overseas Chinese online communities promptly relayed this announcement, while Chinese netizens quickly spread the message in cyberspace through QQ, MSN and other platforms. According to the Anti-CNN site, it received several hundred e-mails that either reported on untrue Western coverage or more generally expressed support for Anti-CNN.

On 21 March 2008, the same day overseas Chinese students were asked to respond to the call for evidence, a public letter from overseas Chinese students referring to the current Western media as "the Nazi German media by Josef Goebbels" was sent to the Western media via publication in a Singaporean online newspaper, which attracted attention around the world (Zaobao.com 2008b). Western media such as Agence France Presse (AFP), Frankfurter Allgemeine Zeitung (FAZ), American National Public Radio (NPR), and the Australian Broadcasting Corporation (ABC) quickly reported the establishment and actions of Anti-CNN.com. At the same time, "Don't be like CNN" became a popular slogan in Chinese cyberspace.

On 27 March 2008, the Chinese Foreign Ministry's regular press conference included a question from a Western journalist asking whether the Chinese government had financed or supported the Anti-CNN website. Qin Gang, the Ministry's regular spokesman, replied,

> What you mentioned displays a social phenomenon that is worth our reflections. You wonder whether Chinese government has been involved. You should take a look at some of the Western coverage. Do you think the social phenomenon needs the Chinese government's stirring up? It is completely the irresponsible and unethical Western reports that infuriated our people to voice voluntarily their condemnation and criticism". (Qin 2008, 27 March)

Qin Gang did not clarify whether the government had initially financed or supported the Anti-CNN website, but his answer, at least seemingly, encouraged Anti-CNN sentiments in China. On 1 April 2008, Chinese Central Television, a major state media source, reported Anti-CNN.com for the first time in a special program, "Warn CNN sternly: why are Chinese netizens angry?" (CCTV.com 2008a). The founder of the website then received a large amount of attention in domestic China. On 13 April, Chinese Central Television broadcast a special interview with the Anti-CNN.com founder entitled "A battle not on your own"(CCTV.com 2008b), and some Chinese netizens praised the founder as a national hero (IDO 2008).

On 18 April 2008, Anti-CNN.com called for official protests after the CNN news commentator Jack Cafferty, in the political program "The Situation Room", described Chinese products as junk, and Chinese people as goons and thugs (Mostrous 2008). The Anti-CNN website provided an official complaint letter in English and Chinese which, it suggested, all Chinese netizens should print, sign and post to CNN's Beijing office. Thousands of Chinese netizens followed the suggestion. Meanwhile, a plan to boycott French goods on China's national public holiday, 1 May, in response to the French boycott of the Olympic Torch Rally in Paris was a point of hot discussion in China. Two days later, on 20 April, Chinese Central Television made another program about Anti-CNN, the theme of the program this time focusing on rationality. The program was entitled "Rationality makes patriotism more powerful" (CCTV.com 2008c). Three days later, Anti-CNN published a letter on its website calling for rational patriotism, which stated plans such as boycotting French goods, burning foreign flags and protesting in front of embassies were irrational and should be controlled (Anti-CNN.com 2008a).

From 13 May through the following month, Anti-CNN's focus shifted to the Sichuan earthquake appeal. On 13 May, 35 hours after the Sichuan earthquake, the Anti-CNN website posted its first multilingual earthquake appeal video invoking Chinese communities worldwide to offer aid. It produced almost 100 videos for the earthquake appeal in one month to 13 June.

After the earthquake appeals, from mid-June 2008, Anti-CNN returned to its focus on Western media bias, revealing numerous examples of Western coverage and advertisements that it considered to contain elements that humiliated China. Later, the website still continued to supply examples from North American and European media sources that, taken overall, it alleged misrepresented China in general. As the website originally stated, this time was a struggle of resistance against Western hegemonic discourse, and the Chinese people should understand the long-term, difficult and complex nature of the fight (see, also, Kennedy 2008).

Anti-CNN members

It is important to note the demographic characteristics of Anti-CNN members during this period. By mid-2009, the Anti-CNN site had 148,967 registered members. According to the personal information the website collected in a member survey at this time (3,976 members responded), the majority were China's Generation Y, only 3 per cent being more than 40 years old and less than 1 per cent above 50 years old. The majority were under 30, and they had also attended college or above (see Figure 6.1).

Anti-CNN members fitted within the general profile of netizens, bloggers, and Generation Y in China. The Anti-CNN website community, therefore, makes an appropriate case site for an examination of the Chinese government's effective use of consumer culture to manage nationalist discourse among Generation Y.

Anti-CNN website responsibilities

In the twelve months after it was founded, Anti-CNN.com fulfilled two roles: timely empowering and restraining of nationalist sentiments. On the one hand, the site gathered evidence of what it considered Western media bias from around the globe and published it in the Anti-CNN forum, thus enabling members to comment and express their anger. On the other hand, the nationalist sentiments once stimulated were in some cases contained when the bloggers' anger became extreme and a potential danger to the state.

This double duty of the Anti-CNN site is evident throughout the course of its growth. From the day the site was founded until mid April 2008, the task of the website was to criticize Western media coverage and call on Chinese netizens' patriotism. Simultaneously, Chinese Central Television's programs sent out the same message, warning CNN sternly and also claiming that the founder of the Anti-CNN website was not on his own in this battle against Western media bias (CCTV.com 2008a).

However, by the end of April, nationalist sentiments had risen to the extreme that some netizens started calling for offline actions, such as boycotting French goods in supermarkets and street protests. At this point, nationalist sentiments expressed online called for restraint. The Anti-CNN site's timely exhortation to the angry Chinese youth to calm down came in the form of a published letter from overseas Chinese to mainland compatriots; this letter encouraged more 'rational' behaviour and patriotic displays. As before, the Chinese Central Television echoed the Anti-CNN's message. The Anti-CNN founder addressed the site's members through a broadcast interview, stating that in order to maintain the stability of the country, protests and campaigns must be stopped:

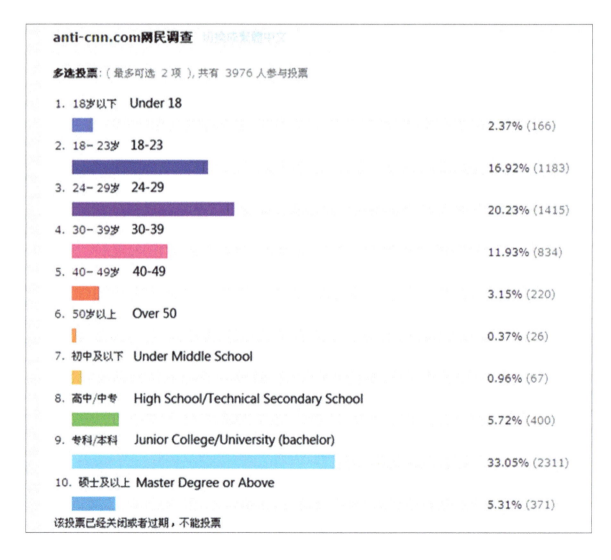

Figure 6.1: Age and education composition of Anti-CNN members
Source:http://www.anti-cnn.com/forum/cn/viewthread.php?tid=12025&highlight=%E7%BD%91%E6%B0
%91%E8%B0%83%E6%9F%A5 (accessed 20 July 2009)

We are very happy that most of our netizens have remained rational and restrained. What we are doing is sending a signal, an attitude, and a warning to those Westerners, who are hostile to China, that they shouldn't ignore the feelings of our 1.3 billion people. But to reduce unnecessary trouble, to avoid giving opportunities to the rioters, to not provide materials for the distorted Western media, we should not be deceived by the hostile group, and campaigns and protests, therefore, must be prohibited. What we need is stability. As our netizens said, we should give our motherland a peaceful sky; we should lessen the burden of our government; we should make law enforcement easier. (Anti-CNN Founder, CCTV.com, 20 April 2008)

The Anti-CNN phenomenon

The Anti-CNN case demonstrates the close ties between nationalism and consumerism in China's cyberspace. It confirms what I argued in Chapter 3, namely, the nationalist sentiments of China's young generations can be manipulated through its increasing reliance on consumerism. But the nationalization of consumerism seen in this case differs from that described by Gerth (2003). Gerth argues that the nationalization of consumerism in China imposes serious constraints on individuals, because it calls for Chinese people to consume products made in China (p. 15), which was a popular call to the previous generation. For Chinese Generation Y, however, loving the motherland does not necessarily prohibit its consumption of products made in the West. In the case of the Anti-CNN site, in particular, Chinese Generation Y's anti-Western sentiments are evidently formed alongside and apart from the new consumer culture.

As I have already argued in previous chapters and in this chapter, nationalism has the potential to become a threat to the Chinese government. Consequently, the Chinese government is handling this phenomenon cautiously by restricting nationalistic sentiment to the domain of consumerism. Consumerism is encouraged — authorized — because it stabilizes society, consolidates power and minimizes any potential threat to the nation-state. I elucidate this explanation in this section with three examples: the spread of the pop song "Don't be like CNN" in cyberspace, the promotion of Anti-CNN sentiments through Chinese "true-man" cyber-shows, and the selling of Anti-CNN products.

The pop song "Don't be like CNN"

In April 2008, a song called "Don't be like CNN", created by one of the Anti-CNN members, was released on the Chinese forums of the Anti-CNN website. It was soon popular with the Chinese youth, partly because the style of the music suited the young generation's taste. The song is in a rap style, and uses Britney Spear's "Baby one more time" as its background music. It was nominated as "the best song in Chinese cyberspace in 2008", and the slogan "Don't be like CNN" was nominated as "the most popular slogan in China in 2008". I translated the lyrics as follows:

> Don't be like CNN/ Western media like bull-shitting/ They unite together to separate Tibet from China; that's their fond dream/ Look at our five-thousand-year-long history/

You are idiots in comparison with us/ You were crawling with your hands/ A piece of bark you call body protection/ Now you pretend to be cool in front us/ You are big, stupid, Western pigs.

Tibet belongs to China/ Dalai Lama wants to separate Tibet from China/ It is us who need to maintain the integrity of our motherland/ How can you foreigners point us directions?/ If you dare walk a step further, we will let you die without a burial place/ China needs to rise up and reunify/ No matter how bitter it is, China needs to/ It will not let Tibet separate.

China is no longer a weak country/ The open reform policy brought us happy life/ We don't allow you to snatch any part of our territory/ We look down upon you/Tibet belongs to China; nothing else needs to be said/ We are a populous country with 1.3 billion brothers and sisters/ Our spit will drown you/ Deutsche Welle, CNN, and BBC, you are a bunch of idiots/ The Chinese are not to be mocked or messed around. (Jiang 2009)

The song itself became extremely popular as a piece of entertainment, but through its three minutes and thirty seconds satiric description of the Western media, China's Generation Y was also consuming its extreme anti-Western and Sino-centric sentiments.

The promotion of the "C" Gesture through online "True-Man" shows

The second example I present here is the promotion of Anti-CNN sentiment through a popular form of online entertainment in China, online "true-man" shows. Almost every social networking website in China has a section of online true-man shows. On these shows, individual netizens post photos of themselves in cyberspace. Posting photos became popular among the young generation because it provides opportunities for finding beautiful girls and good-looking boys, and making friends offline. On the Anti-CNN site, Chinese netizens created the photographic pose called the "C" gesture, which expressed their angry feelings towards Western media and encouraged other netizens to post photos of themselves making the gesture.

Using the "C" gesture in photo-posts to true-man shows is a passionate form of nationalism for Chinese bloggers, enabling them as individuals to show community of spirit in consumerist settings. In effect, nationalist sentiments are being channelled through consumer culture. As one of the initiators of the "C" gesture said,

CNN has reported Chinese domestic affairs in a hostile manner many times, and distorted the truth. It is obviously done to interfere in our domestic affairs. Although we have been developing fast recently, we don't deserve jealousy. So to express my strong protest against CNN, I, a little girl, am here posting my private photo in this discussion forum to attract everybody's attention to boycott CNN together (see Figure 6.2).

This girl's appeal attracted significant attention. Her post received more than 700 replies. Remarkably, though, most of the comments she received did not concern the Anti-CNN sentiments as she had anticipated, but her as an individual: for example, "You have beautiful skin", "Your earrings are so big", "Pretty girl", and "Looking forward to more of your photos" (see Figure 6.3).

Figure 6.2: Anti-CNN "C" gesture of online true-man show
Source: http://tt.mop.com/club/read_2284360.html (accessed 21 July 2009)

Figure 6.3: Examples of comments on the C gesture
Source: http://tt.mop.com/club/read_2284360.html (accessed 21 July 2009)

In this instance, use of the "C" gesture displays the complicated connection between consumerism and nationalism in China. Nationalist discourse is not the focus as such, but Chinese Generation Y is consuming and interacting with nationalism along with all the economic and other social consumerism that interests it. Hence, consumer culture in Chinese cyberspace, which the government encourages, in effect authorizes nationalist discourse. Personal freedom, nationalism and stability are empowered through the promotion of Chinese people's consumer identities. But how deeply does this nationalism penetrate?

Chinese nationalism

The Anti-CNN website has forums in Chinese and English. Content analysis of posts and comments from these forums demonstrates that the website contributors view any negative Western coverage on China as hostile.

In the English forum, of the nineteen discussion boards, three have numerous posts: 'Western Media Bias', 'The Facts of Tibet', and 'Comments and Discussions'. The three discussion boards share the same theme. The Western Media Bias board posts examples of biased Western coverage gathered worldwide; The Facts of Tibet board attempts to prove that Western coverage of Tibet is untrue by posting what posters consider to be the facts, and; Comments and Discussions includes posts from Westerners and domestic Chinese discussing coverage alleged to be biased. I now consider the focus of postings on the Western Media Bias board, the board focusing exclusively on Western media bias, on the Anti-CNN website English forum.

I collected posts over one month, from 18 April 2008 to 18 May 2008. Based on this sample, what the Chinese bloggers consider biased I categorize as four types: politicizing events, and negative, misleading and one-sided news. It was interesting also to note that Chinese bloggers compared the Western reports with Chinese Central Television news and other propaganda machinery in China in order to judge whether a Western report was biased. They argued bias in three ways:

1. If news reported by the Western media was not reported by the Chinese media, then the Western media was biased because the news was untrue and the Western media was racist. For example:

   Sample No. 71 (26/04): *Follow up — the story of the American being attacked is fake*

   Anti-CNN members' comments: The item couldn't be confirmed on Chinese domestic media; therefore, it's another distortion.

2. If negative news reported by the Western media was reported by the Chinese media as well, then the Western media was still biased because it consistently focused on flaws. For example:

   Sample No. 55 (26/04): *CNN's anti-Chinese campaign — CNN special: Made in China*

   Anti-CNN members' comments: CNN focuses on flaws again.

3. If positive news reported by the Chinese media was not reported by the Western media, then the Western media was biased. For example:

Figure 6.4: Guideline of the leading discussion board of Anti-CNN Chinese forum
Source: http://www.anti-cnn.com/forum/cn/ (accessed 20 July 2009)

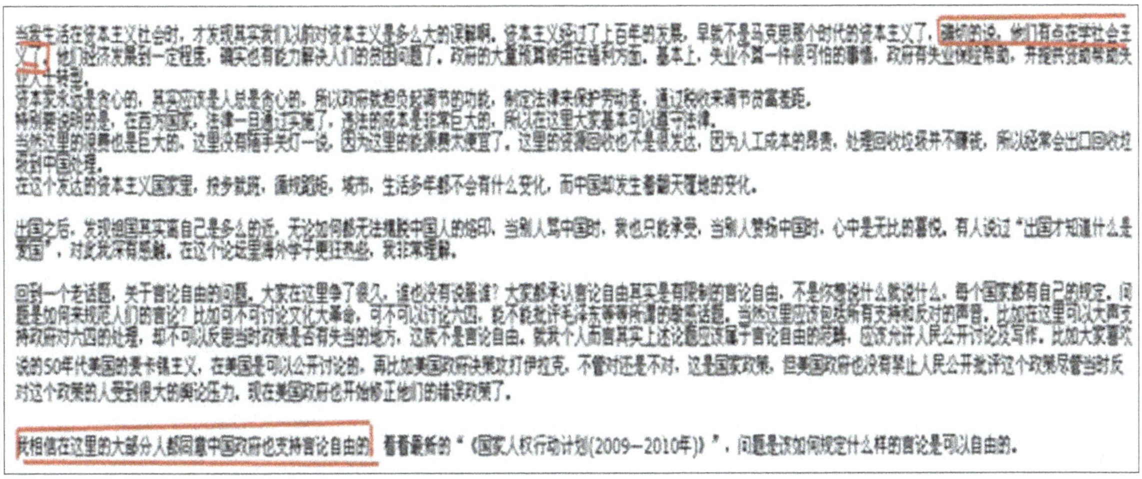

Figure 6.5: An example of political posts on Anti-CNN Chinese forum with a positive tone
Source: http://www.anti-cnn.com/forum/cn/thread-156863-1-2.html (accessed 20 July 2009)

Figure 6.6: Example of posts on democracy
Source: http://www.anti-cnn.com/forum/cn/thread-156560-1-2.html (accessed 21 July 2009)

<u>Sample No. 60</u> (18/04): *Pictures in China, but not yet in the West (3) — Lhasa*
Anti-CNN members' comments: Biased Western media, because the pro-China photos on CCTV were not shown in the Western media.

The Chinese bloggers' criteria indicate the importance of follow-up investigation into media conflicts and misunderstanding between China and the West, but that is not this book's focus. It is important to note here, however, the Anti-CNN website members' belief in the Chinese government any time there is a difference between Western broadcasts and state media coverage in China. Their trust is clearly illustrated in the Chinese version of the forum on the Anti-CNN site.

In the Chinese forum, one discussion board was far ahead of others at the time of data collection, with more than 1,000 daily posts in contrast to less than 50 posts on average per day on other discussion boards. Most of the posts on this discussion board are political. They include discussions of the corruption of government officials, democracy, and government policies. At the same time, as the website itself concludes, the tone of the posts collected was "patriotic, open, positive, passionate and rational, national and international" (see Figure 6.4).

Hence, although this discussion board tends to contain topics that are by nature negative and sensitive, such as those about government officials' corruption and freedom of expression, all the posts at the time of my research were positive about the government. For example, a post entitled "My personal experience and opinion on freedom of expression and the election system" stated that, according to the writer's experience of living in the West as an overseas Chinese person, Western capitalism was actually learning from socialism, and he believed that the Chinese government supported freedom of expression (see Figure 6.5).

The postings on democracy, however, mainly indicated how unsuitable Western democracy was for Asian countries (see Figure 6.6). For example, a post entitled "If this is Western democracy, I'd rather not have it!" pasted photos of violence between a policeman and anti-government protesters in Thailand in April 2009.

Thus, the content analysis of the Anti-CNN forum strengthens the argument of Chapter 2. Nationalist discourse in China proves that political topics are no longer taboo, especially in cyberspace where Chinese netizens appear to have some political freedom albeit within clearly understood limits. Nationalist discourse that politicizes, nationalizes and encourages the consumer culture in Chinese cyberspace fits within these limits. In these spheres, the Chinese are personally empowered through adopting identities as consumers.

Consuming nationalism

The Anti-CNN website, like most sites in Chinese cyberspace, encourages consumer spending despite the nationalist, political character of its creation. In addition to encouraging nationalist debate, it sells nationalistic products. On its one-year anniversary, the website released products targeted at its members. In less than 10 days, there were more than 300 orders for the products (Anti-CNN.com 2008b). These offers included memorial books, T-shirts, computer mouse pads, and bags, each with references to Anti-CNN and at affordable

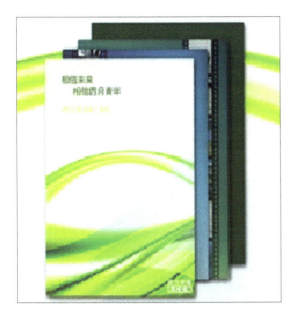

Figure 6.7(a): Memorial book of Anti-CNN, priced at 16 Chinese Yuan (US$1.80)
Source: http://www.anti-cnn.com/forum/cn/thread-149649-1-1.html (accessed 22 July 2009)

Figure 6.7(b): Anti-CNN DIY T-shirt, priced at 36 Chinese Yuan (US$5)
Source: http://www.anti-cnn.com/forum/cn/thread-149649-1-1.html (accessed 22 July 2009)

Figure 6.7(c): Anti-CNN mouse pad, priced at 12 Chinese Yuan (US$1.50)
Source: http://www.anti-cnn.com/forum/cn/thread-149649-1-1.html (accessed 22 July 2009)

Figure 6.7(d): Anti-CNN handbag, priced at 36 Chinese Yuan (US$5)
Source: http://www.anti-cnn.com/forum/cn/thread-149649-1-1.html (accessed 22 July 2009)

prices for individuals wanting to identify with the website and its national perspective (see Figure 6.7).

Commercializing Anti-CNN, then, has two linked implications, first, finance and second, identity. The Anti-CNN website owners pursued commercialization because it would make them money, and Anti-CNN members desired to purchase the products to personally identify with the site. In this case, nationalist discourse has empowered consumerist discourse; the focus on nationalism has again led to influencing the young generation politically, but as consumers rather than citizens seeking voting rights.

Shaping citizens as consumers

Examples such as the Anti-CNN website phenomenon display how netizens' identities can be influenced. Because the consumer culture in cyberspace has the support of the Chinese government, consumerism would seem to be one of its goals for the people. As a governing strategy, it is a means of both encouraging and controlling nationalism.

The Chinese government's development of the Internet has been largely influenced by its potential for commerce and, therefore, its capacity to support national economic growth. At the same time, the government is cautious about allowing free access to e-technology because an unregulated cyberspace might undermine the power and authority of the CCP. Hachigian (2001, p. 118) describes the government's Internet strategy as tripartite in that it encourages economic growth and some personal freedom yet contains potentially unregulated use of cyberspace by both exploiting and controlling its best characteristics. The development of the Internet in China is very much more than a popular communication tool open to everyone. The government endorses its popular use as a means of encouraging a consumer culture and the economic return it can bring with it. The government realizes that individual users must be granted enough cyber freedom to communicate and spend, that too much control will only kill individuals' desire to go online (Tai 2006, p. 97) and so restrain national growth. When Chinese netizens embrace consumerism, the government praises them for supporting the national economy. Being a consumer for China (Qiu 2003, p. 18) is a patriotic duty.

In such ways, freedom to speak online has developed. Political topics are no longer prohibited when they centre on nationalism and pride in China. Meanwhile, the young have become independent online consumers (Powell & Cook 2007) whose interests are channelled to purchase and socialize. Buying for China consumes young people's interest. They feel free, and, indeed, have a measure of freedom not available to previous generations. Generation Y's appreciation of, and gratitude for, its burgeoning economic and social liberty restrain its desire to seek political liberty, so there is no need for direct control. Instead, any political interventionist strategies are diverted from major entities such as national political organizations to smaller, more local communities (Rose 1999, pp. xxi–xxii). These micro-locales implement political control using indirect strategies of governance common to more liberal democratic groupings (Rose and Miller 2001).

7

The Current Political Framework in China: Consolidation or Change?

We, the post-80s of China, grew up with the ideological conflicts between the East and the West; we have very complicated ideological experience, but this has confirmed our love for our nation-state, because we all know, without our nation-state, we wouldn't have the happy life we are having now. What makes the Westerners scared is not the appearance of a patriotic generation, but the appearance of a generation who have independent thought, who love their country with rationality. (Anti-CNN Founder, CCTV.com, 2008c)

Consolidation *and* change

Compared with previous generations, Chinese people enjoy many freedoms, which are evidence of societal change. These freedoms are mainly personal rather than political, however, even though the liberties Chinese people now enjoy as Internet users also allow slightly more extensive freedom to discuss political matters than previously, as the research in this book has shown. Empowered by online consumerist discourse, netizens now have opportunities to debate in cyberspace the issues that matter to them. On the whole, these do not include political matters, except when these matters necessitate the demonstration of the national loyalty so emphatically demonstrated in the bloggers' episode in which Chinese Generation Y, the main users of Chinese cyberspace, registered their anger at Western media's analyses of censorship mechanisms in current China. The government was happy to allow, as this book argues, these demonstrations of national loyalty (see the epigraph above, for example). The collusion between the young generation and the government in this episode suggests very strongly that radical political change, such as the shift from an authoritarian to a democratic government, is not likely to take place anytime soon in China.

As this book has portrayed, the current generation of young Chinese, Generation Y, was the first to grow up in the time of economic reform in China resulting from governmental policy that opened it up to the outside world. This generation was the first in China born after the sudden switch from Maoism to hedonism. As only children, due to China's modern one child per family policy, members of the young generation have been referred to as the "sun" in the family, that is, at its centre, well-fed and over-protected (*People's Daily* 2008). Again, compared with previous generations, Generation Y has been encouraged to develop a consumerist ideology alongside the expansion of Internet technology and better education opportunities. Consequently, this generation has had better opportunities to explore the world with many young Chinese studying overseas following graduation from college or high school.

National loyalty

Against this background of modern change and consolidation, the epigraph to this chapter conveys two messages from China's Generation Y to the rest of the world:

1. The Generation Y of China, which grew up during Deng Xiaoping's economic reforms and the opening up of China to the West, loves China firmly and deeply. Its strongest priority is to maintain the stability of the country. In other words, to assist the government anchor the existing political framework is central to how it interprets "loving one's country".

2. Anti-Western sentiments are embedded in Generation Y's consciousness, even though this generation is regularly exposed to Western culture, possibly even living in the West as well as embracing a Western style of life. Because Generation Y members consider themselves independent thinkers, they can be explicit about who their friends and enemies are. They have this clarity because they trust the Chinese government and believe it has provided them with "the happy life".

The seeming contradictions

What I have paid most attention to in this book are two contradictions: first, between this new generation's embrace of Western culture along with its dislike of Western ideology, and; second, its general political apathy alongside its passionate patriotism. At the same time as the case study of Chinese blogging practice in this book demonstrates young people's apathy towards politics, the case study of the Anti-CNN website presents their anti-Western hostility. The young Chinese generation, although it actively embraces the West, is also proud of what China has accomplished and so resents Western criticism of its country.

The events mentioned in this book also have to be interpreted against the background of China's general enthusiasm for a market economy and the Internet, which, as my analysis has shown, is fundamentally characterized by liberalization *and* control. Within the contradictory context this book identifies, the anger of China's Generation Y towards Western media makes sense. It also becomes possible to understand why common Western assumptions about the political implications of the Internet in China — for example, their perceptions of the role of the Chinese government in shaping the young generation's anti-Western sentiments —

take the form they do. Although I have argued in this book that the freeing of space for political debate in China's cyberworld seems to be an early sign of forthcoming political liberalism, I have counter-argued that this limited political freedom is not likely to bring political democracy to China in the foreseeable future. I have further claimed that the strategy the government has adopted to shape the young generation's anti-Western sentiments — for example, Chinese bloggers' anger towards the Western media — has been to encourage self-regulation, what Foucault has termed the "technologies of the self" (1998a). Uniquely, and therefore interestingly in China's case, this could be called managed (that is, regulated) self-regulation. Specifically, the CCP's strategy has been to stimulate nationalist discourse through encouraging a consumerist culture that gives individuals personal freedoms and a sense of personal empowerment via the consumer identities that they are encouraged to construct. This book, therefore, illuminates a complex paradox of the patriotism of China's Generation Y angered at Western criticisms of anti-democratic practices as well as that generation's adoption of western consumerism *and* the intricacy of — the mutual dependence between — the Chinese government's strategy of liberalization and control to shape Generation Y's engagement with the West.

The political reality

This book has tried to show that Chinese bloggers' anger at Western media criticism of censorship practices in China is the intricate product of three factors, the first largely owing to government intervention, however subtle or indirect at times, and the second and third the results of differences of understanding and experience between China and the West:

1. *Loyalty*: Government endorsement of Generation Y's increasing consumerism has stirred nationalist sentiments.
2. *The benign face of censorship*: The majority of China's Generation Y does not see censorship of their freedom to speak as personally threatening because they have personal economic freedom, for example, in cyberspace.
3. *Apathy towards political freedom:* Chinese enthusiasm for personal economic freedom does not imply a corresponding desire for political liberty, as it almost certainly would in the West.

Thus, China's Generation Y and Western media have different expectations of the political reality of current developments and domestic changes in China.

Liberalism and Chinese government tactics

Despite early signs of political liberalization in Chinese cyberspace, the seemingly liberal environment of China's Internet cannot be simply considered a sign of impending political democratization, because political democracy would require structural changes. As is evident in China, considerable liberalization can take place within an existing political framework. The Internet has brought signs of political liberty to China's cyberspace, but these signs are only early signs, ones that can flourish, as they are doing, within an existing political framework.

In reality, the areas in Chinese cyberspace in which netizens exercise freedom of speech are predominantly apolitical, and among them those areas which do expand from apolitical to political topics function to legitimate and stabilize the existing political framework. An era of governing a young generation, Generation Y, which is mostly cyber-focused, requires different strategies — Foucault's technologies — from those required with previous generations of young people. Generation Y's distinctive, potentially contradictory, characteristics, that is, its self-centredness and rebelliousness, has impelled the Chinese government to govern more indirectly. As noted, indirect technologies regulate the economic and social conduct of individuals and institutions without destroying their distinct or autonomous identities (compare Miller & Rose 1990, p. 88). Yet a government may pass a law centrally which makes it possible for it to influence the development of local activities at a distance over several generations (Latour 1987, p. 232). Direct strategies of governance, such as state censorship, then, are only needed from time to time to supplement indirect strategies determined on a case by case basis by the central government. Thus, although Generation Y is free to pursue its individual desires, the so-called free areas of action are actually controlled by the Chinese government's other tactics, for example, its stimulation of expressions of nationalism through its empowerment of consumer culture online. By shaping Generation Y's core identity as that of the independent consumer, the government is simultaneously determining young people's reliance on the state.

The Chinese central party's governance practices are prime examples of liberties finely calibrated within a non-liberal regime. To put it simply, the government calculates the amounts of personal liberty needed to maintain people's loyalty to the state. The success of its calculations enables it to govern in apparently enlightened, non-coercive ways within the unchanging and powerful framework of an authoritarian regime. Thus, although China's Generation Y is allowed freedoms of actions which have liberal characteristics, the loyalties to the state which these freedoms stimulate, at the same time, stabilize and strengthen the present regime. So while China is labelled a non-liberal country, for the current young generation of China with its everyday freedoms, which include a certain grade of freedom to speak about political matters, China is as liberal as everyone wants (Bennett 2003, p. 62). Despite the existence of disciplinary mechanisms and the exercise of centralized power, as I have demonstrated in the discussions on censorship throughout this book, the government's real power lies in its ability to indirectly manage the self-governing capacities of individuals in Chinese society.

Nevertheless, this book offers only a glimpse into the paradoxical feelings among China's Generation Y concerning the West, as well as the seemingly contradictory strategies the Chinese government has employed to develop its Internet capacity and engage with the West in the market-place. I am most aware of the fact, for example, that the everyday life of Generation Y cannot be generalized according to this glimpse and that the exercise of government may as often be variable as consistent — necessarily so if a government is to be responsive as well as stable. As part of the case analyses included in this book, however, I have sought to identify and illustrate what may prove to be important themes in China as the country in the long term, through its young generation engaging with electronic communication and international trade.

In order to do this, I considered a range of supporting literature. The discipline areas included Chinese and English sources in China studies, Asian studies, Internet studies, political science, sociology and anthropology, complementing the primary research data I gathered from Chinese cyberspace. These data together formed the base for the analyses in Chapters 2, 5 and 6 of this book, enabling me to examine the implications of the social uses of the Internet in China for political structural reforms in this country and to comprehend how seemingly liberal developments in China are actually occurring without the state having to abandon its non-liberal characteristics.

The following conclusions emerged as important themes during the research undertaken for this book.

Most Generation Y members in China do not desire democracy

Chinese bloggers' anti-Western sentiments enflamed online by Western media criticism of censorship in China suggest that China is not ready for structural political reforms. While since the founding of the PRC in 1949, nationalism in China has always contained a strong anti-foreign sentiment, the latest wave of nationalism expressed by China's Generation Y has demonstrated a new anti-foreign element, namely, that democracy is undesirable.

Contrasting concepts of censorship in China and the West

Chinese bloggers' anger at Western criticisms of Chinese censorship practices demonstrates a major difference in understanding between China and the West. As the historical survey in this book of Chinese traditions of censorship from the Song Dynasty when publishing became a thriving enterprise in China to present-day China with its hybrid media landscape has highlighted, Chinese people are actually enjoying considerably more freedom of speech than in the past. The West's lack of understanding of the historical background to China's censorship practices is a major factor in Chinese bloggers' hostility towards Western media and the latter's insensitivity to Chinese cultural values.

Contrasing concept of consumerism in China and the West

Consumerism currently dominates social change in China, particularly in cyberspace, where being a consumer is now highly valued and encouraged. But consumerism is not a Chinese word, and what is special and bewildering about China is that the country operated according to totally opposite ideologies before the birth of consumerism. In three decades, the country has swung from the puritanism of Maoist doctrine in the 1970s to anti-materialism campaigns in the 1980s and then in the late 1990s to the sudden flourishing of hedonism (Qiu 2003). As a consequence, while consumerism is exploited by the government it is at the same time not trusted. The Chinese state allows and empowers its people as consumers on the one hand while on the other it constructs sophisticated managing strategies, as I have shown, in Chinese cyberspace. Chinese consumers are both self-regulating and regulated.

Future directions

Research interest in the fundamental question of whether the Internet will bring democracy to China has been growing for many years, particularly outside China. So far two major approaches to the study of the political implications of the Internet in China have emerged: first, how the Internet is controlled in China; and, second, the use of the Internet in China for democratic or politically dissident purposes. Most analyses take the desire for democracy in China for granted and proclaim the democratic potential of the Internet in China. Paralleling Internet studies, studies of Chinese nationalism have paid attention to the complex interrelationship of nationalism, the state, and democratization in China, particularly in the 1990s, and have pointed out the non-compatibility of nationalism and democracy when it comes to China's national boundary problems (Chang 1998; Friedman 1997; He & Guo 2000, Yu 1996; Sautman 1997). But in their analyses, these researchers and commentators again mainly take Chinese people's desire for democracy for granted in order to admit the democratic potential of nationalism in China (He 2003; Wang 2003). Although recent studies have moved beyond simply predicting whether the Internet or nationalism will help or hinder the development of democracy in China, the approaches of these studies reveal the positive attitudes towards democracy that is basically informed by the assumptions of Western ideologies.

In this book, without denying the assumptions of Western ideologies, I have generally adopted a more concrete approach to analysis. For example, it was not inappropriate to take the desire for democracy for granted before the latest wave of Chinese nationalism, because Chinese nationalists' desire for democracy has been apparent since Deng came to power after Mao's death. However, the new wave of Chinese nationalism represented by China's Generation Y born since the 1980s has shown a different attitude towards democracy. The latest wave of Chinese nationalism, therefore, may subvert rather than advance the previous positive findings on the democratic potential of the Internet in China.

Aligned with this new direction, future research might focus on four areas that, I believe, are under-researched and deserve critical attention. They are as follows:

- *the clash between Western and Chinese media protocols*, extant since the origin of the mass media in different parts of the world and still operating independently since globalization
- *ordinary citizens' political participation in Chinese cyberspace*, which is still in its infancy
- *the online search for relationships,* for example, the phenomenon of the human flesh search engine, which illustrates social interaction as a virtual community in a digital world dominated by new technologies
- *the widening division between netizens and non-netizens, and the latter's exclusion from contemporary Chinese society*, an important factor in examining whether the Internet can bring an authoritarian country to democracy.

In addition to these four research directions, I am excited by the possibility of considering the liberal practices of Chinese governmentality as a source of enrichment for

Western governmentality. The widely employed government practices of liberating areas of activity for China's young generation seem not to be undermining the current political framework but instead to be consolidating it. I therefore find it pertinent and timely to ask this research question: *How can the practice of this new strategy of governance, implemented through a new generation in modern China, contest and enrich governmentality theories in Western theoretical paradigms?* Above all, this book has employed the Western governmentality theories to reveal internal paradoxes in the practice of governance in the Chinese context. It has also demonstrated the benefits of shifting the analytic focus from the representation of China as a sovereign power to a pastoral power.

As this book makes clear, nationalist sentiments can be stimulated through consumerism using subtle censorship mechanisms. In this way, liberalism and governance are constantly entangled. This continuing entanglement makes structural change in current China unlikely but, at the same time, it cannot simply be ruled out as a future possibility. All that is possible for researchers to aim for is to encapsulate and articulate the dynamics of a national state such as China as a growing, living organism and to interpret government actions in the mixed world environment in which it exists.

Appendices

Appendix 1: Examples of headlines of the BBC and in *The New York Times*

BBC

Date	Section	Headline
31 Dec 08	Asia-Pacific	China town given survey answers
16 Dec 08	Asia-Pacific	China's internet 'spin doctors'
12 Dec 08	Asia-Pacific	Cyber crime attack from the East
26 Nov 08	Click	Reaction: Chinese killer executed
20 Nov 08	Asia-Pacific	Peru bets on China's economic muscle
01 Aug 08	Asia-Pacific	China lifts more internet curbs
28 Jul 08	Technology	China becomes biggest net nation
25 Mar 08	Asia-Pacific	China's battle to police the web
29 Aug 07	Technology	Virtual police patrol China web
28 Aug 07	Asia-Pacific	Yahoo plea over China rights case
12 Jun 07	Asia-Pacific	Yahoo's China policy rejected
18 Dec 06	Technology	Net giants 'still failing China'
07 Nov 06	Asia-Pacific	'Enemies of the internet' named
14 Feb 06	Technology	Party elders attack China censors
27 Jan 06	Asia-Pacific	Why Google in China makes sense
06 Jan 06	Technology	The great firewall of China
29 Dec 05	Asia-Pacific	Top Chinese press editor sacked
20 Oct 05	Asia-Pacific	E Asia 'toughest for journalists'
07 Sep 05	Technology	Yahoo helped jail China writer
19 Aug 05	Asia-Pacific	China's breakneck media revolution
14 Jul 05	Asia-Pacific	China curbs media joint ventures
07 Jun 05	Click	Chinese blogs face restrictions
30 Apr 05	Technology	Breaking down the Great Firewall

30 Apr 05	Asia-Pacific	Breaking down the Great Firewall
08 Mar 05	Asia-Pacific	China's tight rein on online growth
31 Aug 04	Asia-Pacific	Chinese newspaper editor freed

The New York Times

Date	Headline
25 Mar 09	YouTube Blocked in China, Google Says
12 Mar 09	A Dirty Pun Tweaks China's Online Censors
16 Feb 09	At Reading in Beijing, Noted Writer Is Stabbed
05 Feb 09	Chinese Learn Limits of Online Freedom as the Filter Tightens
23 Dec 08	China Unblocks The Times's Web Site
17 Dec 08	China Is Said to Restore Blocks on Web Sites
01 Oct 08	Surveillance of Skype Messages Found in China
24 Aug 08	Slipping Over the Great Firewall of China
04 Aug 08	Beijing Under Wraps
02 Aug 08	Olympic Organizers to Weigh Unblocking More Web Sites

Appendix 2: Coverage on Tibet in Chinese Cyberspace

Appendix 3: Topics containing "Tibet" as a key word in Strong Nation Forum

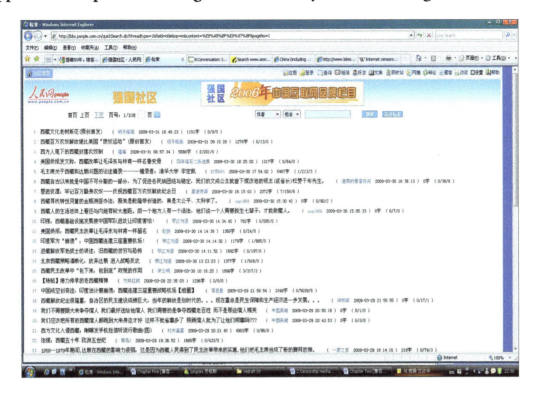

Appendix 4: Homosexual topics on Baidu

Bibliography

Abbott, J. P. 2001. Democracy@internet.asia? The challenges to the emancipator potential of the net: Lessons from China and Malaysia. *Third World Quarterly* 22, 99–114.

Aitken, R. 2007, 28 February. Notes on the Canadian exception: Security certificates in critical context (Paper presented at the Annual Meeting of the International Studies Association, 48th Annual Convention, Chicago, USA). http://www.allacademic.com/meta/p178747_ind ex.html, viewed 16 June 2009.

Albow, M., & Holland, F. 2008. Democratizing global governance (pp. 251–81). In J. Walker & A. S. Thompson (eds), *Critical mass: The emergence of global civil society*. Wilfrid Laurier University Press, Waterloo.

Alex. 2006, 10 March. Massage milk censored. http://www.museumofhoaxes.com/hoax/weblog/permalink/massage_milk_censored/, viewed 18 May 2009.

Amnesty International 2006, 1 February. Human rights and the Internet in China. http://www.amnestyusa.org/document.php?id=ENGUSA200602 01001, viewed 22 May 2009.

Anderson, B. 1991. *Imagined communities: Reflections on the origin and spread of nationalism*. Verso, London.

Anderson, K. 2005, 30 April. Breaking down the Great Firewall, *BBC News*. <http://news.bbc.co.uk/2/hi/asia-pacific/4496163.stm>, viewed 29 March 2009.

Anonymous. 2005, 10 August. http://chinatopblog.com/?p=6, viewed 23 April 2008.

Anti-CNN.com 2008a, 23 April. Anti-CNN shoufa: Haiwai aiguo huodong zuzhizhe zhi guonei tongbao de lianmingxin [Anti-CNN initial publication: A letter from overseas Chinese patriots to domestic Chinese compatriots]. http://www.anti-cnn.com/forum/cn/viewthread.php?tid=34404&extra=page%3D1%26amp%3Bfilter%3Dtype%26amp%3Btypeid%3D16, viewed 16 April 2009.

Anti-CNN.com 2008b, 18 March. AC yizhousui la, jinianpin huore dinggou zhong [AC website one year anniversary, souvenirs are available]. http://www.anticnn.com/forum/cn/viewthread.php?tid=149649&highlight=%E7%BA%AA%E5%BF%B5%E5%93%81, viewed 23 June 2009.

Ash, R. F. 2003. *Hong Kong in transition: One country, two systems*. Routledge, London.

Asian Truly. 2009, 28 February. Xu Jinglei. http://asiantruly.com/xu-jing-lei, viewed 5 June 2009.

Baidu. 2008, 24 March. No new China, no new life. http://zhidao.baidu.com/question/49261031.html, viewed 25 June 2009.

Baiwai Online. 2006, 25 June. Xu Jinglei: boke nvwang [Xu Jinglei: The blog queen]. http://www.beiwaionline.com/training/ez/news/t20060825_9098.htm, viewed 23 May 2009.

Baker, M. 2001. *China and the Internet: Essential legislation.* Asia Information Associates, Hong Kong.

Baoill, A. O. 2004, 1 July. Weblogs and the public sphere. *North Carolina State University Online Journal,* n.p. http://blog.lib.umn.edu/blogosphere/weblogs_and_the_public_ sphere, viewed 12 September 2006.

Barber, B. 1998–9. Three scenarios for the future of technology and strong democracy. *Political Science Quarterly* 113, 4, 573–89.

Barlow, A. 2007. *The rise of the blogosphere.* Greenwood Publishing, Westport, Connecticut.

Barlow, J. P. 1996, 8 February. A declaration of independence in cyberspace. http://homes.eff. org/~barlow/Declaration-Final.htm, viewed 7 March 2008.

Barry, A., Osborne, T., & Rose, N. (eds), *Foucault and political reason: Liberalism, neo-liberalism and rationalities of government.* London, University College London.

BBC. 2008, 24 September. Du naifen: "Bu neng" haishi "bu wei" [Poisoned milk powder: "Can't" or "don't"]. http://news.bbc.co.uk/chinese/simp/hi/newsid_7630000/ newsid_7634000/7634058.stm, viewed on 2 April 2009.

Besley, T. 2006, *Counseling youth: Foucault, power and the ethics of subjectivity.* Praeger Publishers, Westport, CT.

Bingfeng. 2006, 12 March. Massage milk hoax and "peer pressure" in Western media. http://blog.bcchinese.net/bingfeng/archive/2006/03/12/59423.aspx, viewed 27 January 2009.

Blood, R. 2002. *The weblog handbook: Practical advice on creating and maintaining your blog.* Perseus Publishing, Cambridge, Massachussetts.

Boas, T., & Kalathil, S. 2003. *Open networks, closed regimes: The impact of the Internet on authoritarian rule.* Carnegie Endowment for International Peace, Washington D.C.

Bourdieu, P. 1991. Censorship and the imposition of form (pp. 137–63). In J. B. Thompson (ed.), *Language and symbolic power.* Harvard University Press, Cambridge, Massachussetts.

Bowker, R. R. 1912. *Copyright: Its history and its law. Being a summary of the principles and practices of copyright with special reference to the America code of 1909 and the British act of 1911.* Houghton Mifflin Company, Boston.

Brass, P. R. 1991. *Ethnicity and nationalism: Theory and comparison.* Sage, Newbury Park, California.

Breuilly, J. 1985. Reflections on nationalism. *Philosophy of the Social Sciences* 15, 65–75.

Breuilly, J. 1993. *Nationalism and the state,* 2nd edn. Manchester University Press, Manchester.

Browning, G. 2002. *Electronic democracy: Using the Internet to transform American politics,* 2nd edn. Information Today, Medford, New Jersey.

Bryant, L. 2011, 'Internet powers Tunisian protests', 17 January. http://www.voanews.com/ english/news/africa/Internet-Powers-Tunisian-Protests-113868589.html, viewed 30 January 2012.

Burchell, G. 1991, Peculiar interests: Civil society and governing "the system of natural liberty" (pp. 119–50). In G. Burchell et al. (eds).

Burchell, G. 1996, 'Liberal government and techniques of the self' (pp. 19–35). In A. Barry, T. Osborne & N. Rose (eds).

Burchell, G., Gordon, C., & Miller, P. (eds) 1991. *The Foucault effect: Studies in governmentality*. Harvester Wheatsheaf, Hemel Hempstead, Hertfordshire.

Burt, R. 1994. Introduction: The "New" censorship (p. xi). In R. Burt (ed.), *The administration of aesthetics: Censorship, political criticism, and the public sphere*, University of Minnesota Press, Minnesota.

Burt, R. 1998. (Un)Censoring in detail: The fetish of censorship in the early modern pasts and the postmodern present (pp. 17–43). In C. R. Post (ed.), *Censorship and silencing: Practices of cultural regulation*. The Getty Research Institute for the History of Art and the Humanities, Los Angeles.

Butler, J. 1997. *Excitable speech: A politics of the performative*. Routledge, London.

Buzan, B., & Segal, G. 1994. Rethinking East Asian security. *Survival* 36, 2, 3–21.

Calhoun, C. 1997. *Nationalism*. Open University Press, Buckingham.

Caputo, J. 2006. *Foucault and the Critique of Institutions*. Penn State Press, Pennsylvania.

Caspi, D., & Limor, Y. 1999. *The in/outsiders: The media in Israel*. Hampton Press, Cresskill, New Jersey.

Castells, M. 1997. *The information age: Economy, society and culture. Vol. 2, The power of identity*. Blackwell, Oxford.

CCTV.com. 2008a, 31 March. Zhengao CNN: Wangmin weishenme fennu [Warn CNN sternly: Why Chinese netizens are angry]. http://news.cctv.com/special/C17274/01/20080331/105026.shtml, viewed 15 April 2009.

CCTV.com. 2008b, 13 April. Bushi yigeren de zhandou [A battle not on your own], http://www.cctv.com/video/duihua/2008/04/duihua_300_20080414_1.shtml, viewed 15 April 2009.

CCTV.com. 2008c, 20 April. Lixing rang aiguo geng youli [Rationality makes patriotism more powerful], http://news.cctv.com/china/20080420/102581_4.shtml, viewed 27 April 2009.

Chan, H. L. 1983. *Control of publishing in China, past and present*. Australian National University, Canberra.

Chan, M. K. 1994. From anti-foreignism to popular nationalism: Hong Kong between China and Britain, 1839–1911 pp. 9–25. In M. K. Chan (ed.), *Precarious balance: Hong Kong between China and Britain, 1842–1992*. Hong Kong University Press, Hong Kong.

Chang, J. 2003. *Wild swans: Three daughters of China*. Touchstone, Austin, Texas.

Chang, J., & Halliday, J. 2005. *Mao: The unknown story*. Jonathan Cape, London.

Chang, M. H. 1998. Chinese irredentist nationalism: The magician's last trick. *Comparative Strategy* 17, 1, 83–101.

Chang, T. H. 1999. *China During the Cultural Revolution*. Greenwood Publishing, Westport, Connecticut.

Chase, M. 2002. *You've got dissent! Chinese dissent use of the Internet and Beijing's counter-strategies*. RAND, Santa Monica, California.

Chen, H., & Chan, J.M. 1998. Bird-caged press freedom in China (pp. 645–69). In J. Y. S.

Chang (ed.), *China in the post-Deng era*. The Chinese University Press, Hong Kong.

Chen, L. 2002, 15 July. Wo jiushi duanxin wenhua de muhou heishou [I am a backstage manipulator of SMS culture]. *Xin Zhou Kan* [New Weekly], Guangzhou, 39.

Chen, S. M. 1996. Min zu zhu yi: Fu xing zhi dao? [Nationalism: a way for revival?]. *DF* 2, 74–6.

Chen, Y. 1992, June. *Publishing in China in the post-Mao era: The case of Lady Chatterley's lover.* Asian Survey 32, 6, 568–82.

Cherrington, R. 1991. *China's students: The struggle for democracy.* Routledge, New York.

Chin, J. 2009, 9 June. Revolution? No thanks. I am busy shopping. *Global Post.* http://www.globalpost.com/dispatch/china-and-its-neighbors/090608/chinas-silent-campuses, viewed 19 June 2009.

China.com.cn. 2007, 20 April. Shichangbao: Wangluo saohuang, guizai chijiu [Market newspaper: Lasting crackdown is the key to stop online porn]. http://www.china.com.cn/policy/zhuanti/wlsq/2007-04/20/content_8144892.htm, viewed 31 March 2009.

China Daily. 2003, 4 April. The epidemic of atypical pneumonia known as the severe acute respiratory syndrome (SARS) in China has been put under control ... http://www.chinadaily.com.cn/en/doc/2003-04/04/content_160716.htm, viewed 29 March 2009.

China Daily. 2005, 3 June. A sexual revolution silently going on in China. http://www.chinadaily.com.cn/english/doc/2005-06/03/content_448407.htm, viewed 3 April 2009.

China Daily. 2009, 31 March. China shuts down 162 websites containing lewd videos. http://www.chinadaily.com.cn/china/2009-03/31/content_7634223.htm, viewed 31 March 2009.

China Digital Times. 2005, 24 June. Translation of the filtered key words in Chinese cyberspace. http://chinadigitaltimes.net/2005/06/translation-of-the-filtered-key-words-in-chinese-cyberspace/, viewed 23 May 2005.

Chinageny.com. 2006 [n.d.], About the book. *China's Generation Y* (China's Generation Y official book site). http://www.chinageny.com/html/main.html, viewed 23 June 2009.

Chinalaw.gov.cn. 2004, 23 August. Zuigao renmin fayuan, zuigao renmin jianchayuan, gonganbu guanyu kaizhan daji yinhui seqing wangzhan zhuanxiang xingdong youguan gongzuo de tongzhi [Announcement of launch of special operation by law to crack down on online lewd and porn content]. http://www.chinalaw.gov.cn/article/fgkd/xfg/cfjs/200408/20040800039975.shtml, viewed 31 March 2009.

Chinasarft.gov.cn. 2007, 29 December. New regulations for online audio and video services. http://www.chinasarft.gov.cn, viewed 13 April 2008.

Christensen, T. 1996, September/October. Chinese Realpolitik. *Foreign Affairs* 75, 5, 37–40.

Clinton, B. 2000, October. Speech (delivered at Paul H. Nitze School for Advanced International Studies at Johns Hopkins University, 8 March). In S. Kalathil, W. J. Drake, & C. B. Taylor (eds), *Dictatorships in the digital age: Some considerations on the Internet in China and Cuba — Information Impacts.* http://www.cisp.org/imp/october_2000/10_00drake.htm, viewed 11 November 2008.

CNNIC. 2005, 27 September. Decree on the management of Internet news/information services. http://www.cnnic.org.cn/html/Dir/ 2005/09/27/3184.htm, viewed 13 March 2009.

CNNIC. 2006, 6 November. A brief introduction of CNNIC (pp. 15–6). In CNNIC, *Survey report on search engine market in China*. http://www.cnnic.cn/download/2006/yinqing06menu_en.pdf, viewed 23 June 2009.

CNNIC. 2007a, 15 February. Statistical reports on the Internet development in China: the 19th survey report. http://www.cnnic.cn/index/0E/00/11/index.htm, viewed 7 March 2009.

CNNIC. 2007b, 26 December. CNNIC releases 2007 survey report on China weblog market number of blog writers reaches 47 million equalling one fourth of total netizens. http://www.cnnic.cn/html/Dir/2007/12/27/4954.htm, viewed 28 March 2007.

CNNIC. 2008a, 15 August. Glossary-Netizens. In *Statistical survey report on the Internet development in China: The 22nd survey report*. http://www.cnnic.cn/download/2008/CNNIC22threport-en.pdf, viewed 6 March 2009.

CNNIC. 2008b, 6 March. Statistical reports on the Internet development in China: The 21st survey report. http://www.cnnic.cn/index/0E/00/11/index.htm, viewed 7 March 2009.

CNNIC. 2009, 23 March. Statistical reports on the Internet development in China: The 23rd survey report. http://www.cnnic.cn/index/0E/00/11/index.htm, viewed 7 May 2009.

Cody, E. 2007, 28 June. Text messages giving voice to Chinese: opponents of chemical factory found way around censors, *Washington Post*. http://www.washingtonpost.com/wp-dyn/content/article/2007/06/27/AR2007062702962.htm, viewed 1 April 2009.

Cohen, M. 2001. *Censhorship in Canadian Literature*. McGill, Queen's Press, Quebec.

Connor, W. 1994. *Ethnonationalism: The quest for understanding*. Princeton University Press, Princeton, New Jersey.

Cullen, R., & Choy, P. D. W. 1999. The Internet in China. *Columbia Journal of Asian Law* 13, 1, 99–134.

Davis, D.S. (ed.) 2000. *The consumer revolution in urban China*. University of California Press, Berkeley.

Dean, M. 1991. *The constitution of poverty: Toward a genealogy of liberal governance*. Routledge, New York.

Dean, M. 1999. *Governmentality: Power and rule in modern society*. Sage, London.

Dean, M. 2002. Liberal government and authoritarianism. *Economy and Society* 31, 1, 37–61.

Deibert, R. 2002. Dark guests and great firewalls: The Internet and Chinese security policy. *Journal of Social Issues* 58, 1, 143–59.

Deibert, R., Palfrey, J., Rohozinsik, R., & Zittrain, J. (eds) 2008. *Access denied: The practice and policy of global Internet filtering*. The MIT Press, Cambridge, Massachusetts.

Delanty, G., & Kumar, K. 2006. *The SAGE handbook of nations and nationalism*. SAGE, Thousand Oaks, California.

Deng, X. P. 1995. *Selected works of Deng Xiaoping: 1975–82*, vol. 2. Foreign Languages Press, Beijing.

Dillon, M. (ed.) 1998. *China: A historical and cultural dictionary*. Routledge, London.

Dittmer, L., & Kim, S. (eds). *China's quest for national identity*. Cornell University Press,

Ithaca, New York.

Dittmer, L., & Kim, S. 1993. Whither China's quest for national identity? (pp. 237–91). In L. Dittmer & S. Kim (eds).

Donald, S. H. & Keane, M. 2002. Media in China: New convergences, new approaches (pp. 3–17). In S. H. Donald, M. Keane & Y. Hong (eds), *Media in China: Consumption, content and crisis*. Routledge, London.

Doyle, M. 1983. Kant, liberal legacies, and foreign affairs: Parts I & II. *Philosophy and Public Affairs* 12, 3, 205–35, and 12, 4, 323–53.

Dutton, M. 2008. The passions of governmentality. *Postcolonial Studies* 11, 1, 303–14.

EastSouthWestNorth. 2007, 1 June. The Xiamen PX project. http://zonaeuropa. com/20070601_1.htm, viewed 2 April 2009.

Ebrey, P. B. 1993. *Chinese civilization: A sourcebook*. Free Press, Ohio.

Elegant, S. 2007, 26 July. China's me generation. *The Times*. http://www.time.com/time/ magazine/article/0,9171,1647228-1,00.html, viewed 26 August 2007.

Eudaily, S. P. 2004. *The present politics of the past: Indigenous legal activism and resistance*. Routledge, New York.

Felix, L., & Stolarz, D. 2003. *Hands-on guide to video blogging and podcasting*. Focal Press, Burlington, Maine.

Ferdinand, P. (ed.) 2000. *The Internet, democracy and democratization*. Frank Cass, London.

Fishman, T. C. 2005. *China, Inc: How the rise of the next superpower challenges America and the world*. Scribner, New York.

Fitzgerald, A., 2011, 'Protests manifest in Egypt, organized through social media sites', 27 January. http://www.business2community.com/trends-news/protests-manifest-in-egypt-organized-through-social-media-sites-011868, viewed 30 January 2012.

Fong, V. 2004. Filial nationalism among Chinese youth with global identities. *American Ethnologist* 3, 1, 629–46.

Ford, P. 2008, 28 November. China's virtual vigilantes: Civic action or cyber mobs? *The Christian Science Monitor*. http://www.csmonitor.com/2008/1128/p01s01-woap.html, viewed 8 June 2009.

Foster, W. 2000. *The diffusion of the Internet in China*. Stanford University, Stanford, California.

Foucault, M. 1973. *The birth of the clinic: An archaeology of medical perception*. Pantheon, New York.

Foucault, M. 1976. *The history of sexuality, vol 1: The will to knowledge*. Penguin, London.

Foucault, M. 1977. *Discipline and punish: The birth of prison*. Vintage, New York.

Foucault, M. 1983. Afterword: The subject and power (pp. 208–26). In H. L. Dreyfuss & P. Rabinow, *Michel Foucault: Beyond structuralism and hermeneutics*, 2nd edn, University of Chicago Press, Chicago.

Foucault, M. 1984. *The history of sexuality, vol. 3: The care of self*. Penguin, London.

Foucault, M. 1988a. Technologies of the self (pp. 16–49). In L. H. Martin, H. Gutman, & P. H. Hutton (eds), *Technologies of the self: A seminar with Michael Foucault*. The University of Massachusetts Press, Amherst.

Foucault, M. 1988b. Politics and Reason (pp. 57–85). In L. Kritzman (ed.), *Michel Foucault: Politics, philosophy, culture*. Routledge, London.

Foucault, M. 1991. Governmentality (pp. 87–104). In G. Burchell et al. (eds).

Foucault, M. 1992. *The history of sexuality, vol. 2: The use of pleasure*. Penguin, London.

Foucault, M., Burchell, G., Gordon, C., & Miller, P. 1991. *The Foucault effect: Studies in governmentality, with two lectures by and an interview with Michel Foucault*. University of Chicago Press, Chicago.

Fowler, G. A., & Qin, J. 2006, 14 March. Chinese bloggers stage hoax (p. B3). *Wall Street Journal*.

Francis, C. B. 1989. The progress of protest in China: The spring of 1989. *Asian Survey* 29, 898–915.

French, P. 2007, 8 March. Asia-Pacific: consumerism — China's iPod revolution. *Ethical Corporation*. http://www.ethicalcorp.com/content.asp?ContentID=4925, viewed 28 April 2008.

Friedberg, A. L. 1993/1994. Ripe for rivalry: Prospects for peace in a multipolar Asia. *International Security* 18, 3, 5–33.

Friedman, E. 1997. Chinese nationalism, Taiwan autonomy and the prospects of a larger war. *Journal of Contemporary China* 6, 14, 5–33.

Frontline 2003 [n.d.]. China and the Internet. http://www.pbs.org/wgbh/pages/frontline/shows/red/roundtable/internet.html, viewed 30 May 2009.

Gandy, O. H., Jr. 1993. *The panoptic sort: A political economy of personal information*. Western Press, Boulder, Colorado.

Gary, S. 2006. *Governing Chinese bodies: The discourse of population from plan to market*. Edward Elgar, Cheltenham, Gloucestershire.

Gellner, E. 1983. *Nations and nationalism*. Basil Blackwell, Oxford.

Gerth, K. 2003. *China made: Consumer culture and the creation of the nation*. Harvard University Press, Cambridge, Massachusetts.

Gillham, B. 2000. *Case study research methods*. Continuum International Publishing Group, London.

Global Voices Online 2009, 1 April. China: Tightening control over Internet audio-visual content. http://advocacy.globalvoicesonline.org/2009/04/01/china-tightening-control-over-internet-audio-visual-content/, viewed 30 April 2009.

Goldkorn, J. 2006a, 8 March. Blocking blogs: The cowardice of China's net nanny. http://www.danwei.org/media_and_advertising/blocking_blogs_the_cowardice_o.php, viewed 21 July 2008.

Goldkorn, J. 2006b, 9 March. Massage Milk's disappearance: An April Fool's joke. http://www.danwei.org/media_and_advertising/massage_milks_disappearance_an.php, viewed 18 May 2009.

Goldkorn, J. 2006c, 27 April. Danwei TV 7: Muzi Mei sex blogger. http://www.danwei.org/danwei_tv/danwei_tv_7_mu_zimei_interview.php, viewed 23 April 2009.

Goldsmith, J. & Wu, T. 2006. How governments rule the Net (pp. 65–87). In J. Goldsmith & T. Wu (eds), *Who controls the Internet: Illusions of a borderless world*, Oxford University

Press, New York.

Gordon, C. 1991. Introduction (pp. 1–51). In G. Burchell et al. (eds).

Gries, P. H. 2004. *Chinese new nationalism: Pride, politics, and diplomacy*. University of California Press, Berkeley.

Gries, P. H. 2005. Nationalism and Chinese foreign policy (pp. 103–20). In Y. Deng & F. L. Wang (eds), *China rising: Power and motivation in Chinese foreign policy*, Rowman & Littlefield, Lanham, Maryland.

Grossman, L. K. 1995. *The electronic republic: Reshaping democracy in America*. Viking, New York.

Gutstein, D. 1999. *E.con: How the Internet undermines democracy*. Stoddart, Toronto.

Guy, R. K. 1987. *The Emperor's four treasuries: Scholars and the state in the late Ch'ien-lung*. Harvard University Press, Cambridge, Massachusetts.

Hachigian, N. 2001, March/April. China's cyber-strategy. *Foreign Affairs* 80, 2, 118–33.

Hachten, W. A., & Hachten, H. 1996. *The world news prism: Changing media of international communication*, 4th edn. Iowa State University Press, Ames, Iowa.

Hamrin, C. L., & Zhao, S. 1995. *Decision-making in Deng's China: Perspectives from insiders*. M. E. Sharpe, New York.

Harris, E. 2002. *Nationalism and Democratization: Politics of Slovakia and Slovenia*. Ashgate, Burlington, Vermont.

Hartford, K. 2000, September. Cyberspace with Chinese Characteristics. *Current History*. http://china-wired.com/pubs/ch/home.htm, viewed 11 March 2009.

He, B. 2003. China's national identity: A source of conflict between democracy and state nationalism (pp. 170–92). In L. H. Liew & S. Wang (eds), *Nationalism, democracy and national integration in China*, Routledge, London.

He, B., & Guo, Y. 2000. *Nationalism, national identity and democratization in China*. Ashgate, Aldershot, Berkshire.

Hewitt, D. 2007. *Getting rich first: Life in a changing China*. Chatto & Windus, London.

Hill, D. T., & Sen, K. 2005. *The Internet in Indonesia's new democracy*. Routledge, London.

Hill, K. A., & Hughes, J. E. 1998. *Cyberpolitics: Citizen journalism in the age of the Internet*. Rowman & Littlefield, Lanham, Maryland.

Hindess, B. 2001a. The liberal government of unfreedom. *Alternatives* 26, 257–72.

Hindess, B. 2001b. Democracy as Anti-Democracy. *Southern Review* 34, 1, 9–21.

Hobsbawm, E. 1983. Introduction: The invention of tradition (pp. 1–14). In E. Hobsbawm & T. Ranger (eds), *The invention of tradition*, Cambridge University Press, Cambridge.

Hoffman, L. 2006, November. Autonomous choices and patriotic professionalism: On governmentality in late-socialist China. *Economy and Society* 35, 4, 550–70.

Hong, J. 1998. *The internationalization of television in China: The evolution of ideology*. Greenwood Publishing Group, Westport, Connecticut.

Hsu, I. 1960. China's entrance into the family of nations: The diplomatic phase, 1858–1880. Harvard University Press, Cambridge, Massachusetts.

Hu, J. 2002, 27 November. Rights group looks at China and tech. *CNET News*. http://news.cnet.com/Rights-group-looks-at-China-and-techs/2100-1023_3-975517.html, viewed 31 March 2009.

Hughes, C. R. 2000, Spring/Summer. Nationalism in Chinese cyberspace. *Cambridge Review of International Affairs* 13, 2, 195–209.

Hughes, C. R. 2003. *China and the Internet: Politics of the digital leap forward*. RoutledgeCurzon, New York.

Hughes, C. R. 2006. *Chinese nationalism in the global era*. Routledge, London.

Iboysky.com 2009, 31 March. 5000 wan zhongguo tongzhi zheng zaoyu aizi xiji [50 million Chinese gay are being attacked by HIV]. http://www.iboysky.com/inews/antihiv/200903/25296.shtml, viewed 31 March 2009.

IDO 2008, 26 March. Minzu yingxiong: Zui xian fanji waimei waiqu lasa shijianzhe raojin [The National hero: The first Chinese stroke back to Western distorted coverage on Lhasa — Rao Jin]. http://ido.3mt.com.cn/Article/200803/show933923c30p1.html, viewed 15 June 2009.

ISC 2002, 19 July. Public pledge of self-regulation and professional ethics for China Internet industry. http://www.isc.org.cn/20020417/ca102762.htm, viewed 13 March 2009.

IT Facts 2008, 28 April. U.S. Internet users demographic profile in March 2008. http://www.itfacts.biz/us-internet-users-demographi c-profile-in-march-2008/10440, viewed 11 March2009.

Jacobs, C. 2009, 19 March. Leaked government blacklist confirms worst fears. *Electronic Frontiers Australia*. http://www.efa.org.au/2009/03/19/leaked-government-blacklist-confirms-worst-fears/, viewed 30 May 2009.

Jansen, S. C. 1991. *Censorship: The knot that binds power and knowledge*. Oxford University Press, New York.

Jayasuiya, K 2007. *Asian regional governance: crisis and change*. Routledge, London.

Jeffrey, L. 2000. *China's wired: Your guide to the Internet in China*. Asia Law & Practice, Hong Kong.

Jeffreys, E. 2004. *China, sex and prostitution*. Routledge, London.

Kalathil, S. 2001. *The Internet and state control in authoritarian regimes: China, Cuba, and the counterrevolution*. Carnegie Endowment for International Peace, Washington, D.C.

Kalathil, S. 2002. 'Community and communalism in the information age', *The Brown Journal of World Affairs*, 9, 1, 347–54.

Karl, R. E. 2002. *Staging the world: Chinese nationalism at the turn of the twentieth century*. Duke University Press, Duke, N Carolina.

Keane, J. 1991. *The media and democracy*, Wiley Publishing, Queensland.

Keane, M., Hemelryk, D. S., & Hong, Y. (eds) 2002. *Media in China: Consumption, content and crisis*. RoutledgeCurzon, London.

Kedourie, E. 1994. *Nationalism*, 4th edn. Blackwell, Oxford.

Kellas, J. G. 1991. *The politics of nationalism and ethnicity*. Macmillan, London.

Kennedy, J. 2007, 18 May. China: Citizen blogger treading new ground. *Globalvoices online*. http://www.globalvoicesonline.org/2007/05/18/china-citizen-blogger-treading-new-ground/, viewed 13 May 2009.

Kennedy, J. 2008, 24 March. China: bloggers declare war on Western media's Tibet coverage.

Global Voices Online. http://globalvoicesonline.org/2008/03/24/china-bloggers-declare-war-on-western-medias-tibet-coverage/, viewed 20 March 2009.

Kerner, S. M. 2005, 10 August. Blog readers spend more time and money online. *The ClickZ Network.* http://www.clickz.com/showPage.html?page=3526591, viewed 23 April 2008.

Klang, M., & Murray, A. (eds) 2005. *Human rights in the digital age.* Glasshouse Press, London.

Kluver, A. R. 1996. *Legitimating the Chinese economic reforms: a rhetoric of myth and orthodoxy.* SUNY Press, New York.

Kongqixibo 2009, 3 March. Zhenshi yu huangyan de you yici boyi: Toushi xifang meiti dui 3.14shijian de xujia baodao [Another battle against lies: Dissecting Western media's fake information on the 3/14 incident]. *Anti-CNN.com.* http://www.anti-cnn.com/forum/cn/viewthread.php?tid=145479&highlight=%E8%A5%BF%E6%96%B9%E5%AA%92%E4%BD%93, viewed 20 March 2009.

Kraus, R. C. 2004. *The party and the arty in China: The new politics of culture.* Rowman & Littlefield, Lanham, Maryland.

Kristof, N. D. 1993. The rise of China. *Foreign Affairs* 72, 5, 59–73.

Kristof, N. D. 2005, 24 May. Death by a thousand blogs. *The New York Times,* 21, Section A, Column 1.

Kurlantzick, J. 2004, 5 April. Dictatorship.com: The web won't topple tyranny. *The New Republic,* 21–5.

Lagerkvist, J. 2006. *The Internet in China: Unlocking and containing the public sphere.* Media-Tryck, Lund, Sweden.

Lankshear, C., & Knobel, M. 2006. *New literacies.* Open University Press, New York.

Lasica, J. D. 2003. Blogs and journalism need each other. *Nieman Report* 57, 3, 70–4.

Latham, K. 2007. *Pop culture China!* ABC-CLIO, Oxford.

Latour, B. 1987. *Science in action: How to follow scientists and engineers through society.* Harvard University Press, Cambridge, Massachusetts.

Lawrence, A. 1998. *China under Communism.* Routledge, London.

Levenson, J. L. 1964. *Modern China and its Confucian past: The problem of intellectual continuity.* Anchor Books, New York.

Li, C. 1998. *China: The consumer revolution.* John Wiley & Sons, New York.

Li, L. 2008, 28 February. The "ME" generation. *Beijing Review.* http://www.bjreview.com.cn/special/post-1980s_in_earthquake/txt/2008-02/03/content_132879.htm, viewed 13 March 2009.

Liang, Q. 1959. *Xinmin shuo* [On new citizenship]. Zhonghua Shuju, Taipei.

Liang, Q. 1989a. Zhongguoshi xulun [A narrative analysis of Chinese history]. In *Yinbingshi heji 1,* p. 3, Zhongguo Shuju, Beijing.

Liang, Q. 1989b. Zhongguo liguo zhi dafangzhen [The fundamental policies for China's being a nation-state]. In *Yinbingshi heji* 4, 39–78, Zhongguo Shuju, Beijing.

Lim, M 2006, 'The polarization of identity through the Internet and struggle for democracy in Indonesia', CIOS, 1 July, viewed 30 January 2012, http://www.cios.org/www/ejc/

v143toc.htm.

Limor, Y., & Nossek, H. 2000. The "monkey trial" in the land of the bible: Modern techniques of religious censorship — the case study of Israel (pp. 63–78). In J. Thierstein & Y. Kamalipour, (eds), *Religion, law, and freedom: A global perspective*, Greenwood Publishing Group, Westport, Connecticut.

Lin, Y. 1979. *The crisis of Chinese consciousness*. The University of Wisconsin Press, Madison, Wisconsin.

Lingfengwangzi 2008, 26 August. Beijing aoyun: Xifang meiti de shibai he chiru [Beijing Olympics: Shame and humiliation for Western media]. *Anti-CNN.com.* http://www.anti-cnn.com/forum/cn/viewthread.php?tid=94128&highlight=%E8%A5%BF%E6%96%B9%E5%AA%92%E4%BD%93, viewed 20 March 2009.

Link, P. 2008, 18 June. A short anatomy of Chinese nationalism today. www.uscc.gov/hearings/2008hearings/transcripts/08_06_18trans/link.pdf, viewed 20 March 2009.

Lu, W., Du, J., Zhang, J., Ma, F., & Le, T. 2002. Internet development in China. *Journal of Information Science* 28, 3, 207–33.

Lyon, D. 2003. Cyberspace, surveillance, and social control: The hidden face of the Internet in Asia. In K. C. Ho, R. Kluver, & K. C. C. Yang (eds), *Asia.com.asia encounters the Internet*. RoutledgeCurzon, London and New York.

Ma, E. 2000. Rethinking media studies: The case of China (pp. 21–34). In J. Curran & M. J. Park (eds.), *De-westernizing media studies*. Routledge, London.

Mackinnon, R. 2005, 7 November. Chinese bloggers: Everybody is somebody. *Rconversation.* http://rconversation.blogs.com/rconversation/2005/11/page/2/, viewed on 13 June 2009.

Mackinnon, R. 2006, 14 March. The great Chinese censorship hoax. *Rconversation.* http://rconversation.blogs.com/rconversation/2006/03/the_great_chine.html, viewed 26 February 2009.

MacKinnon, R. 2007. Flatter world and thicker walls? Blogs, censorship and civic discourse in China. *Public Choice* 134, 31–46.

Mackinnon, R. 2008, 26 March. Anti-CNN and the Tibet information war. *Rconversation.* http://rconversation.blogs.com/rconversation/2008/03/anti-cnn-the-me.html, viewed 25 February 2009.

Mackinnon, R. 2009a, 2 February. China's censorship 2.0: How companies censor bloggers. *First Monday* 14, 2. http://firstmonday.org/htbin/cgiwrap/bin/ojs/index.php/fm/article/view/2378/2089, viewed on 23 June 2009.

Mackinnon, R 2009b, 26 February. Internet control without "firewalls". *RConversation.* http://rconversation.blogs.com/rconversation/2009/02/internet-control-without-firewalls.html, viewed 31 March 2009.

Marbridge Daily 2007, 29 December. SARFT, MII co-issue online video regulation. http://www.marbridgeconsulting.com/marbridgedaily/2007-12-29/article/7063/sarft_mii_co_issue_online_video_regulation, viewed 29 June 2009.

Martin, L., Gutman, H., & Hutton, H. (eds) 1988. *Technologies of the self: A seminar with Michel Foucault*. Tavistock Publications, London.

McGuigan, J. 1996. Censorship and moral regulation (154–75). In J. McGuigan, (ed.), *Culture and thePublic Sphere*. Routledge, London.

McQuail, D 1994, *Mass communication theory*, SAGE publications, London.

Mengin, F. 2004. *Cyber China: Reshaping national identities in the age of information*. Palgrave Macmillan, New York.

Min Q. 1989. *Zhongguo zhengzhi wenhua* [Political culture in China]. Kunming, Unnan renmin chubanshe.

Miller, N. 2002. *China's Internet regulatory environment*. IDC Research, Framingham, Maine.

Miller, P., & Rose, N. 1990. Governing economic life. *Economy and Society* 19, 1, 75–105.

Miller, T. 1993. *The well-tempered self: Citizenship, culture, and the postmodern subject*. The Johns Hopkins University Press, Baltimore.

Miller, T. 1998. *Technologies of the truth: Cultural citizenship and the popular media*. University of Minnesota Press, Minneapolis, Minnesota.

Morgan Stanley. 2005, September 12. China Internet: creating consumer value in digital China. http://www.morganstanley.com/institutional/techresearch/pdfs/China_ Internet_091205.pdf, viewed 13 March 2009.

Mostrous, A. 2008, 16 April. CNN Apologizes to China Over "thugs and goons" comment by Jack Cafferty. *Times Online*. http://www.timesonline.co.uk/tol/news/world/ article3756437.ece, viewed 23 April 2008.

Mueller, M. & Tan, Z. 1997. *China in the information age: Telecommunications and the dilemmas of reform*. The Washington Papers/169. Praeger, Westport, Connecticut.

Muller, B. 2004. Censorship and cultural regulation: mapping the territory (pp. 1–32). In B. Muller (ed.), *Censorship and cultural regulation in the modern age*. Rodopi, Amsterdam.

MySinchew. 2008, 1 September. China's "ME" generation finally focuses on us. http://www. mysinchew.com/node/15545, viewed on 14 April 2009.

NCCT. 2006, 1 October. Regulations of the People's Republic of China for safety protection of computer information systems. http://www.ncctac.org/article_content.asp?unid=410, viewed on 29 April 2009.

NetEaseNews. 2008, 23 October. Shanghai nanzishaoqianxianfu [Shanghai man burning money to show off his richness]. http://news.163.com/06/1023/17/2U4R9BGQ00011229. html, viewed 27 April 2009.

Neveu, E. 2004. Government, the state and media (pp. 331–50). In G. Downing, D. McQuail, E. Wartella, & P. Schlesinger (eds), *The SAGE handbook of media studies*. SAGE, London.

New York Times. 2003, 30 November. China's celebrity sex columnist, <http://www. nytimes.com/2003/11/30/world/internet-sex-column-thrills-and-inflames-china. html?pagewanted=all&src=pm>, viewed on 31 January 2012.

Nonini, D. 2008. Is China becoming neoliberal? *Critique of Anthropology* 28, 2, 145–76.

Norton Online Living Report. 2009. Adults kids online activities. http://www. nortononlineliving.com/documents/NOLR_Report_09.pdf, viewed 23 July 2009.

O'Donnell, G., & Schmitter, P. C. 1986. *Transitions from authoritarian rule:Prospects for democracy*. The John Hopkins University Press, Baltimore, Maryland.

Okamoto, S. 1996. *Shindai kinsho no kenkyu* [Research on prohibited books in China].Tokyo Daigaku Shuppankai, Tokyo.

Open Net Initiative. 2009, 15 June. Country profiles: China. http://opennet.net/research/profiles/china, viewed 23 June 2009.

Owen, J. M. 1994. How liberalism produces democratic peace. *International Security* 19, 2, 87–125.

Ozikirimli, U. 2000. *Theories of nationalism: A critical introduction.* Palgrave Macmillan, Hampshire, UK.

Pan, P. 2006, 18 February. Keywords used to filter web content [n.p.]. *Washington Post.* http://www.washingtonpost.com/wp-dyn/content/article/2006/02/18/AR2006021800554.htm, viewed 14 April 2009.

Pei, M. 2006a. *China's trapped transition: The limits of developmental autocracy.* Harvard University Press, Cambridge, Massachusetts.

Pei, M 2006b. The dark side of China's rise. *Foreign Policy* 253, 32–40.

People.com.cn. 2009, 23 February. Tencent has the largest social network in the world. http://game.people.com.cn/GB/48644/48662/8849643.html, viewed 03 April 2009.

People's Daily. 2000, 5 August. Chinese Internet police. http://english.peopledaily.com.cn/english/200008/05/eng20000805_47390.html, viewed 23 May 2009.

People's Daily. 2008, 4 June. Complete new appraisal of the Post-80s' generation. http://english.peopledaily.com.cn/90001/90780/91345/6424404.html, viewed 12 March 2009.

People's Daily. 2009, 13 February. Computer scientists offer smarter tool to spot porn websites http://english.peopledaily.com.cn/90001/90776/90881/6592318.html, viewed 20 June 2009.

Philips, P., & Harslof, I. 1997. Censorship within modern democratic societies (pp. 1–14). In P. Phillips (ed.), *Censored 1999: The news that didn't make the news.* Seven Stories Press, New York.

Poboo.cn. 2006, 18 June. 2006 boke baobei dasai [2006 blog babe competition]. *www.poboo.cn/baby/fa.asp*, viewed 12 May 2009.

Post, C. R. 1998. Censorship and silencing (pp. 1–17). In C. R. Post (ed.), *Censorship and silencing: Practices of cultural regulation.* The Getty Research Institute for the History of Art and the Humanities, Los Angeles.

Powell, J. L., & Cook, I. G. 2000. A tiger behind and coming up fast: Governmentality and the politics of population control in China. Journal of Aging and Identity 5, 2, 79–89.

Powell, J. L., & Cook, I. G. 2007. New perspectives on China and aging. Nova Publishers, New York.

Project Cleanfeed Canada. 2006, 24 November. ISPs and tipline set up battle against Internet child exploitation. http://www.cybertip.ca/en/cybertip/cleanfeed_canada, viewed 20 April 2009.

Pye, L. 1996. How China's nationalism was Shanghaied (pp. 86–112). In J. Unger (ed.), *Chinese nationalism.* M.E. Sharpe, Armonk, New York.

Qi, Y. 2000. The current situation and prospect of Chinese information resources on the

Web. *Social Science Computer Review* 18, 4, 484–9.

Qin, G. 2008, 27 March. 2008 nian 2 yue 27 hao waijiaobu fayanren Qin Gang juxing lixing jizhehui [27th March 2008 Chinese Foreign Ministry spokesperson Qin Gang's regular press conference]. Ministry of Foreign Affairs of the People's Republic of China. http://www.fmprc.gov.cn/chn/gxh/tyb/fyrbt/jzhsl/t418831.htm, viewed 15 April 2009.

Qiu, J. L. 2003, 1 October. The Internet in China: Date and issues (Paper presented at Annenberg Research Seminar on International Communication, Los Angeles). http://arnic.info/Papers/JQ_China_and_Internet.pdf, viewed 25 May 2009.

QQ News 2008, 15 May. Ni maiguo ma: Xiaobailing hua xueben mai shenchipin de xinli mimi [Did you ever buy it: The white collars' psychological secret of buying luxuries]. http://finance.qq.com/a/20080515/001429.htm, viewed 10 June 2009.

Robert, D. 1997, 1 January. The new China lobby. The American Prospect. http://www.encyclopedia.com/The+American+Prospect/publications.aspx?date=199701&pageNumber=1, viewed 29 March 2009.

Rose, N. 1998. The crisis of welfare states (pp. 54–87). In S. Hanninen (ed.), *The displacement of social policies*. SoPhi, Jvaskyla.

Rose, N. 1999a. *Governing the soul: The shaping of the private self,* 2nd edn. Free Associations Books, London.

Rose, N. 1999b. Preface to the second edition (pp. xxi–xxii). In N. Rose (ed.), *Governing the soul: The shaping of the private self,* 2nd edn, Free Associations Books, London.

Rose, N., & Miller, P. 1992. Political power beyond the state: Problematic of government. *British Journal of Sociology* 43, 2, 173–205.

Rosen, S. 1991. Youth and social change in the PRC (pp. 288–316). In R. H. Myers (ed.), *Two Societies in opposition: The republic of China and the People's Republic of China after forty years.* Hoover Institution Press, Cliff, Stanford, California.

Rosenfield, S. 2001. Writing the history of censorship in the age of enlightment (pp. 117–45). In D. Gordon (ed.), *Postmodernism and the enlightment: New perspectives in eighteenth-century French intellectual history.* Routledge, London.

Roy, D. 1995. Assessing the Asian-Pacific "power vacuum". *Survival* 37, 3, 45–60.

Russett, B. 1993. *Grasping the democratic peace: Principles for a post-Cold War world.* Princeton University Press, Princeton, New Jersey.

Saco, D. 2002. *Cybering democracy: Public space and the Internet.* University of Minnesota, Minnesota.

Sae, O. 1996. *Shindai kinsho no kenkyu* [Research on prohibited books in China]. Tokyo Daigaku Toyo Bunka Kenkyujo, Tokyo.

Saeys, F. 2007. *Western broadcast models: Structure, conduct and performance.* Walter de Gruyter, Berlin.

Sautman, B. 1997. Racial nationalism and China's external behavior. *World Affairs* 160, 2, 78–96.

Schmidt, J. D. 2003. *Harmony garden: The life, literary criticism, and poetry of Yuan Mei (1716–1798).* Routledge, New York and London.

Schwartz, B. 1964. *In search of wealth and power.* Harper Torchbook, New York.

Segal, G. 1995, September. Rising nationalism in China worries the Japanese. *International Herald Tribune* 28, 10.

Shane, P. M. 2004. *Democracy online: The prospects for political renewal through the Internet.* Routledge, London.

Shapiro, A. 1999. *The control revolution: How the Internet is putting individuals in charge and changing the world as we know it.* Public Affairs, New York.

Sheng, J. 2008 [n.d]. China: SARFT and MII regulations on online video. HubPages. http://hubpages.com/hub/China-SARFT-and-MII-regulations-on-online-video, viewed 28 June 2009.

Siebert, F. 1956. The authoritarian theory (pp. 9–38). In F. Siebert, W. Schramm, & R. Patterson (eds).

Siebert, F., Schramm, W., & Patterson, R. (eds). 1956. *Four theories of the press.* University of Illinois Press, Urbana.

Sigley, G. 2006. Chinese governmentalities: Government, governance and the Socialist market economy. *Economy and Society* 35, 4, 487–508.

Simon, L. D., Corrales, J., & Wolfensberger, D. R. 2002. *Democracy and the Internet: Allies or adversaries?* Woodrow Wilson Center, Washington D.C.

Sinablog. 2009, 3 June, Xu Jinglei de boke [Xu Jinglei's blog]. http://blog.sina.com.cn/u/1190363061, viewed 16 June 2009.

Sina News. 2004, 3 August. Seqing wangluo neixian bai neimu: Shichang xuqiu yinfa "huangwang" fanlan [A insider from porn website: The flood of porn nets is caused by the market demand]. http://news.sina.com.cn/c/2004-08-03/17533916257.shtml, viewed 31 March 2009.

Sina News. 2008, 31 October. Wangyou zicheng renrou sousuo chu weixie nvtong gaoguan [Netizens say high rank official who harassed a female child has been searched out via human flesh search engine]. http://news.sina.com.cn/s/2008-10-31/153716564823.shtml, viewed 6 April 2009.

Smith, A. D. 1991. *National identity.* Penguin, London.

Sohu. 2008, 9 January. Zhuan jia yu ji: 2008 nian zhongguo liu xue ren shu you wang tu po 20 wan [Experts predict: There will be more than 200,000 Chinese go abroad in 2008]. http://business.sohu.com/20080109/n254554676.shtml, viewed 13 March 2009.

Song, Q. & Wang, X. D. 2009. *Zhongguo bu gaoxing* [Unhappy China]. Jiangsu Renmin Chubanshe [Jiangsu People's Publishing], Nanjing, China.

South China Morning Post. 1995, 10 January. China joins Internet and exposes its flank, p. 2.

Stanat, M. 2006. *China's Generation Y: Understanding the future leaders of the world's next superpower.* Homa & Sekey Books, Paramus, New Jersey.

Stevenson, R. L. 1995. Freedom of the press around the world. In J. C. Merrill (ed.), *Global journalism: Survey of international communication*, 3rd edn. Longman, London.

Stokes, E. 1959. *The English utilitarians and India.* Clarendon Press, Oxford.

Su, X. K & Wang, L. X., (eds) 1988. *Heshang* [River Elegy]. Xian dai chu ban she, Beijing.

Sun, L. P. 1996. Huiru shijie zhuliu wenming-minzu zhuyi santi [Flowing together with the world's mainstream civilization]. *DF* 1, 15–19.

Sun, Y. 1991. The Chinese protests of 1989: The issue of corruption. *Asian Survey 31*, 762–82.

Symmons-Symonolewicz, K. 1985. The concept of nationhood: Toward a theoretical clarification. *Canadian Review of Studies in Nationalism XII*, 2, 359–60.

Tai, Z. 2006. *The Internet in China: Cyberspace and civil society.* Routledge, London.

Talbot, S. 1996. Democracy and the national interest. *Foreign Affairs 75*, 6, 47–63.

Tangos. 2007, 3 November. Chinese bloggers conference 2007 in Beijing. *China Web 2.0 Review.* http://www.cwrblog.net/902/chinese-blogger-conference-2007-in-beijing.html, viewed 11 April 2009.

Teiwes, F. C. 1996, March. Seeking the historical Mao. *The China Quarterly* 145, 176–88.

The Guardian. 2007, 20 July. Chinese actor writes world's top blog. http://www.guardian.co.uk/technology/2007/jul/20/news.newmedia , viewed 30 March 2008.

The Standard. 2007, 14 July. Message in a cellphone. http://www.thestandard.com.hk/news_print.asp?art_id=48956&sid=14284850, viewed 25 June 2009.

The World Factbook. 2009, 8 July. East and Southeast Asia: China. https://www.cia.gov/library/publications/the-world-factbook/geos/ch.html, viewed 27 June 2009.

Tilley, V. 1997. The terms of the debate: Untangling language about ethnicity and ethnic movements. *Ethnic and Racial Studies* 20, 3, 497–522.

Timothy, B. 1988. Censorship in eighteenth century China: A review from the book trade. *Canadian Journal of History* 22, 2, 177–96.

Tsui, L. 2001. *Big mama is watching you: Internet control by the Chinese government* (unpublished M.A. thesis). University of Leiden, Leiden.

Tyson, A. 1995. *Chinese awakenings: Life stories from the unofficial China.* Westview Press, Boulder, Colorado.

U.S. House of Representatives Committee on International Relations Subcommittee on Asia and the Pacific. 2006, 15 February. Hearing: The Internet in China — a tool for freedom or suppression? http://wwwc.house.gov/international_relations/aphear.htm, viewed 8 November 2008.

Usher, S. 2006, 8 March. China shuts down outspoken blog. *BBC News.* http://news.bbc.co.uk/2/hi/asia-pacific/4787302.stm, viewed 20 October 2008.

Wang, G. W. 1996. *The revival of Chinese nationalism.* International Institute for AsianStudies, Leiden.

Wang, J. 2008. *Brand new China: Advertising, media, and commercial culture.* Harvard University Press, Cambridge, Massachusetts.

Wang, J. S. 2005, 7 November. BBC's Interview. *Wangjianshuo's Blog.* http://home.wangjianshuo.com/archives/20051107_bbcs_interview.htm, viewed 26 April 2006.

Wang, K. W. (ed.). 1998. *Modern China: An encyclopedia of history, culture, and nationalism.* Garland Publishing, New York.

Wang, S. G. 2003, 30 May. Nationalism and democracy: Second thoughts. www.cuhk.edu.hk/gpa/wang_files/Nationalism&Dem.doc, viewed 7 March 2009.

Wang, P. 2009, 7 September. Xin Qing [mood], blog entry, <http://blog.sina.com.cn/s/blog_49e039890100050r.html>, viewed 15 March 2012.

Wang, Y. 2004. *Urban poverty, housing and social change in China*. Routledge, London.

Washington Post. 2006, 18 February. Keywords used to filter web content. http://www.washingtonpost.com/wp-dyn/content/article/2006/02/18/AR2006021800554.htm, viewed 23 April 2009.

Watts, J. 2005, 14 June. China's secret Internet police target critics with web of propaganda. *The Guardian.* http://technology.guardian.co.uk/online/news/0,12597,1505988,00.html#article_continue, viewed 13 March 2009.

Wei, C. X. G., & Liu, X. Y. 2001. *Chinese nationalism in perspective: Historical and recent cases*. Greenwood Publishing Group, Lanham, Maryland.

Wei, C. X. G., Liu, X. Y., & Kirby, W. C. 2002. *Exploring nationalisms of China: Themes and conflicts*. Greenwood Publishing Group, Lanham, Maryland.

Weiquan Wang [Chinese Human Rights Defenders]. 2008, 10 July. Zhongguo wangluo jiankong yu fanjiankong niandu baogao (2007) [Annual report on Chinese Internet surveillance and actions against surveillance]. http://crd-net.org/Article/Class1/200807/20080710165332_9340.html, viewed 25March 2009.

Wikipedia Contributors. 2004. Trent Lott. *Wikipedia: The free encyclopaedia.* http://en.wikipedia.org/wiki/Trent Lott, viewed 23 June 2006.

Wikipedia Contributors. 2006. Political blogs. *Wikipedia: the free encyclopaedia.* http://en.wikipedia.org/wiki/Political_blog, viewed 28 June 2009.

Wikipedia Contributors. 2008a. Muzi Mei. *Wikipedia: the free encyclopaedia.* http://en.wikipedia.org/wiki/Muzi_Mei, viewed 29 March 2008.

Wikipedia Contributors. 2008b. List of words censored by search engines in the People's Republic of China. http://en.wikipedia.org/wiki/List_of_words_censored_by_search_engines_in_the_People's_Republic_of_China, viewed 23 May 2009.

Wikipedia Contributors. 2009a. Blog. *Wikipedia: The free encyclopaedia.* http://en.wikipedia.org/wiki/Blog, viewed 25 June 2009.

Wikipedia Contributors. 2009b. Blogosphere. *Wikipedia: The free encyclopaedia.* http://en.wikipedia.org/wiki/Blogosphere, viewed 29 June 2009.

Wikipedia Contributors. 2009c. Anti-CNN. *Wikipedia: The free encyclopaedia.* http://en.wikipedia.org/wiki/Anti-cnn, viewed 20 July 2009.

Woesler, M. & Zhang, J. H. 2002. *China's digital dream: The impact of the Internet on the Chinese society.* European University, Singapore.

Womark, B. 1986. *Media and the Chinese public: A survey of the Beijing media audience*. M. E. Sharpe, Armonk, New York.

Wu, Y. 1998. *China's consumer revolution: The emerging patterns of wealth and expenditure*. Edward Elgar, London.

Xi, R. Y. 2006. *The Internet, freedom of speech, and social transformation: An examination of the impact of cyber-forums on policy-making in China*. ProQuest Information and Learning, Michigan.

Xiao, P., Wu, X. J., & Chen, H. N., 2008, 22 April. 700 wan MSN yonghu liang qi aiguo hongxin, zhangxian quanqiu huaren tuanjie [700 Chinese MSN users added the symbol of a red heart against their MSN names and placed the English word "China" next to it, to display the unity of global ethnic Chinese]. http://media.people.com.cn/ GB/40606/7148157.html, viewed 15 March 2012.

Xiao, Q. 2004, 30 August. The words you never see in Chinese cyberspace. *China Digital Times.* http://chinadigitaltimes.net/2004/08/the_words_you_n.php, viewed 15 April 2009.

Xiaolisishen. 2007. Ten types of Chinese blogs. *Review of World Invention* 4, 50–1. http:// www.cqvip.com/asp/vipsearch.asp, viewed on 20 April 2008.

*Yah*oo. 2007, 31 October. "Wangluo yiyeqing" zheng qudai "jiuba yiyeqing" ["Cyber one-night-stand" is replacing "pub one-night-stand"]. http://xk.cn.yahoo.com/ articles/071031/1/5109.html, viewed 23 June 2009.

Yang, G. B. 2009. *The power of the Internet in China:Citizen activism online.* Columbia University Press, New York.

Yao, K. 1979, December. *Sung-chao Tui-yu Shu-pao Ti Kuan-chih vol.1*, pp. 268–80.

York J. 2011, 'Tunisia's taste of internet freedom', *Algazeera*, 14 January. http://www.aljazeera. com/indepth/opinion/2011/01/201111410250537313.html, viewed 30 January 2012.

Young, C. 1976. *The politics of cultural pluralism.* University of Wisconsin Press, Madison, Wisconsin.

Yu, H. Q. 2007, December. Blogging the everyday life in Chinese Internet culture. *Asian Studies Review* 31, 423–33.

Yu, Y. 1996 [n.d.], Minzu yu minzhu zhijian [Between democracy and nationalism]. http:// www.hornbill.cdc.net.my/e-class/culture/democ01.htm, viewed 7 March 2009.

Yujiro, M. 1997, Dynasty, state, and society: The case of modern China (pp. 113–42). In J. A. Fogel & P. G. Zarrow (eds), *Imagining the people: Chinese intellectuals and the concept of citizenship, 1890–1929*, M. E. Sharpe, Armonk, New York.

Zaobao.com. 2008a, 8 March. Zhendui xiamen shimin youxing fandui PX gongchang fujian shuji: Minzhong huanbao yishi qianglie [Regarding the protests against PX factory, Secretary of Fujian Province: Residents are aware of environmental issues]. http://www. zaobao.com/special/npc/pages3/npc080308e.shtml, viewed 2 April 2009.

Zaobao.com. 2008b, 21 March. Zhongguo haiwai liuxuesheng qunqi kangyi xifang meiti duixizang pianmian baodao [Overseas Chinese students united together against the one-sided Western coverage on Tibet]. http://realtime.zaobao.com/2008/03/080321_26a. shtml, viewed 14 April 2009.

Zha, J. Y. 1995. *China Pop.* The New Press, New York.

Zhang, J. L. 2009, 19 January. Wangluo zhengzhi canyu de shidai yijing daodai [The era of online participation has arrived]. *Sichuan Academy of Social Sciences.* http://www.sass. cn/skynews.asp?newsid=7780, viewed 1 April 2009.

Zhang, X. D. 2001. *Whither China? Intellectual politics in contemporary China.* Duke University Press, Durham, North Carolina.

Zhao, D. X. 2002. An angle on nationalism in China today: Attitudes among students after Belgrade 1999. *China Quarterly* 172, 885–905.

Zhao, S. S. 2004. *A nation-state by construction: Dynamics of modern Chinese nationalism.* Stanford University Press, Stanford, California.

Zhao, S. S. 2005, Autumn. Nationalism's double edge. *The Wilson Quarterly.* http://74.125.155.132/search?q=cache:R5fCpvYI6BAJ:www.wilsoncenter.org/index.cfm%3Ffuseaction%3Dwq.print%26essay_id%3D146859%26stoplayout%3Dtrue+nationalism+is+a+double-edged+sword&cd=7&hl=zh-CN&ct=clnk, viewed 29 May 2009.

Zheng, Y. N. 1994, Summer. Development and democracy: Are they compatible in China? *Political Science Quarterly* 109, 2, 35–59.

Zheng, Y. N. 1999. *Discovering Chinese nationalism in China: Modernization, identity, and international relations.* Cambridge University Press, Cambridge.

Zheng, Y. N. 2008. *Technological empowerment: The Internet, state, and society in China.* Stanford University Press, Stanford, California.

Zhongguo Jingji Wang [China Economy Net]. 2009, 6 February. 2001: APEC — "Zhongguo nian" de lishi huazhang [2001: APEC — The historical section of "Year of China"]. http://views.ce.cn/fun/corpus/ce/7/200902/06/t20090206_18138037.shtml, viewed 20 March 2009.

Zhou, J. 2006. *Higher education in China.* Cengage Learning Asia, Singapore.

Zhou, Y. M. 2005a. *Historicizing online politics: Telegraphy, the Internet, and political participation in China.* Stanford University, Stanford, California.

Zhou, Y. M. 2005b. Informed nationalism: Military websites in Chinese cyberspace. *Journal of Contemporary China 14*, 543–62.

Zuckerman, E. 2008, 25 March. Bridgeblogging Chinese anger over perceived media bias. http://www.ethanzuckerman.com/blog/2008/03/25/bridgeblogging-chinese-anger-over-perceived-media-bias/, viewed 23 July 2009.

This book is available as a fully-searchable pdf from
www.adelaide.edu.au/press

www.ingramcontent.com/pod-product-compliance
Lightning Source LLC
Chambersburg PA
CBHW041005050326
40689CB00026B/4983